WHAT WERE THEY AFRAID OF

The Cemetery of the Infants near Lugnano in Teverina

David Soren, Delaney Fisher, Roberto Montagnetti, David Pickel and Jordan Wilson

Sponsored by the Joseph and Mary Cacioppo Foundation

www.innovativeinkpublishing.com
Send all inquiries to:
4050 Westmark Drive
Dubuque, IA 52004-1840

What Were They Afraid Of?
The Infant Cemetery of Poggio Gramignano, Umbria

"I awoke to what felt like lightning going through my legs, and then spreading through my body and in my head. Probably the worst headache, body aches, and chills you could possibly imagine. It felt like I was being stung repeatedly by an electric shock gun and could barely control my movements. The pain was so intense; I actually believed I was dying, literally crying out in pain so bad that I was taken to a 24 hour clinic that night at 3am."[1]

That is an actual contemporary description made by someone suffering symptoms from malaria, as recorded by American business magnate Bill Gates. But what must it have seemed like in ca. A.D. 450 with no clinic and no modern biomedical knowledge of the cause of the terror spreading through a small agricultural community along the Tiber River in Umbria about 65 miles north of Rome between the small towns of Lugnano in Teverina and Attigliano? (Figure 1) It was an event that caused pregnant women to miscarry their unborn infants prematurely and was able to kill small children and likely also their mothers (and fathers) in rapidly increasing numbers.

The epidemic itself, if from *Plasmodium falciparum* malaria as we have suggested in our work, would most likely have displayed itself in an horrific fashion, gestating in perhaps less than a week, and causing, since it was unable to be treated, a myriad of dreadful symptoms including a jaundiced or yellowish appearance, shivering, sweating, increased heart rate, rapid breathing, painfully enlarged spleen and liver, blood-clotting with tiny purple spots on the skin, yellowing of the whites of the eye, redness or bluish quality of the skin, and abdominal distention.[2]

With no understandable answers to this major disease event, the terrified local rural citizenry reverted to traditional beliefs and magic rituals performed by religious leaders instead of to Christian-

FIGURE 1 Map showing the location of the Roman villa.

ity in the hope of mitigating the disease's impact. This article is devoted to attempting to understand the world view of this community in the face of a public health crisis at the intersection of traditional beliefs and Christianity. What happened, how did the citizens respond to it, and what were the local people afraid of?

THE BASIC SITUATION

The event occurred at the site of Poggio Gramignano, a hillside area overlooking the Tiber River which was just a mile or so away and 7 miles from the modern limits of the small town of Lugnano in Teverina in whose territory it lies (Figure 2). Here, in a cemetery devoted entirely to preterm and newborn infants, along with several toddler-aged children and the highly unusual inclusion of an 8 to 12 year old child, were interred individuals over a very short period of time in 59 distinct burials. The ruins at Poggio Gramignano were first discovered in 1984 and recognized as a Roman villa of circa 30 B.C. (Figure 3) but the cemetery installed within the ruins of the villa in the mid fifth century A.D. in Rooms 10 to 12, 15 and 17 was discovered in 1986 by the University of Arizona team (Figure 4). This graveyard was the burial place for victims of what we have postulated to be an epidemic of *Plasmodium falciparum* malaria, suggested after initial hypotheses by the Arizona team and subsequent independent testing by Robert Sallares and Jamie Inwood[3] (Figure 5). Confined to the villa's west-facing rooms, these burials include nine fetuses, 21 perinates, 30 infants under 1 year of age, and two children (one aged 2 to 3 years and one 8 to 12 years); thus the majority range in age from approximately 6 lunar (gestational) months to 1 year.[4]

FIGURE 2 View of Poggio Gramignano at the far back, right of center, from Lugnano in Teverina.

FIGURE 3 Reconstruction of the Roman villa of circa 30 B.C. (overlooking the Tiber River) which was discovered at Poggio Gramignano near the town of Lugnano in Teverina.

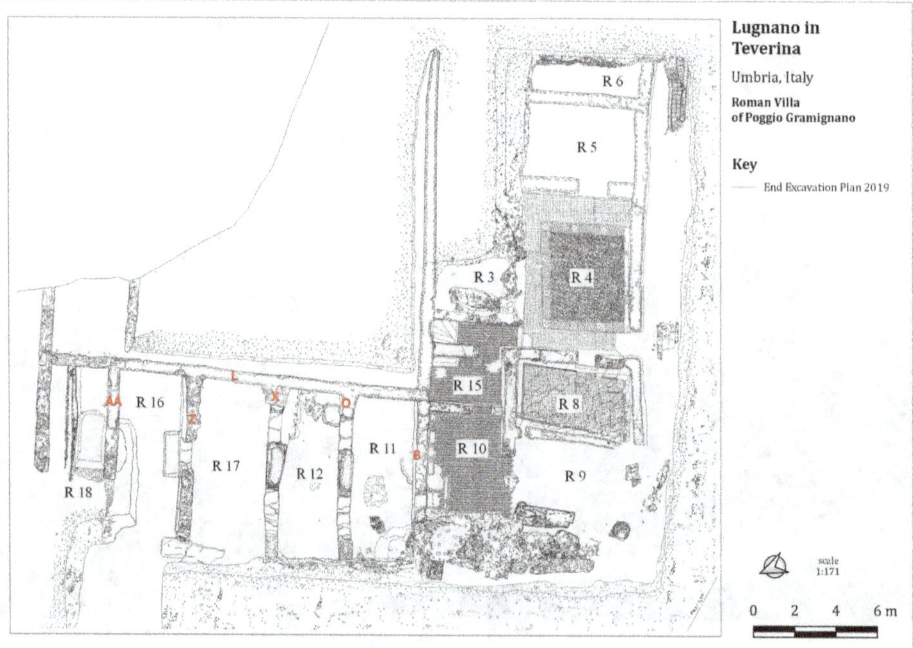

FIGURE 4 Plan of the Roman villa showing the original storage rooms 10 to 12, 15 and 17, which were converted into an infant cemetery in the fifth century A.D.

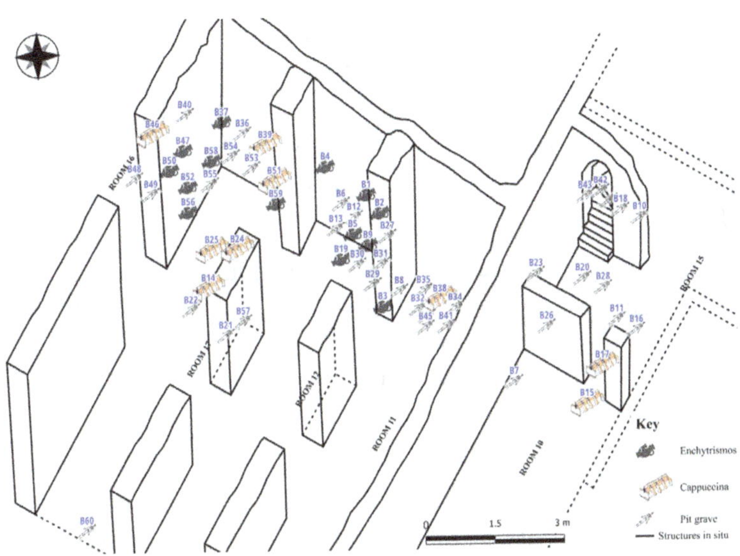

FIGURE 5 Reconstruction view of the infant cemetery area with all 59 burials.

The severity and intensity of this epidemic caused rapidly increasing numbers of deaths for not only fetuses and children but, if our hypotheses are correct, for adults as well. As in areas in which malaria is endemic in the modern day, pregnant women were likely the most severely affected. It took the community by surprise. In the absence of adult remains, it is difficult to estimate the mortality caused by this disease event, though modern examples give us an idea since even in 2021 there were over 619,000 deaths world-wide, of which 77% were children under five years of age. The deaths at the Poggio Gramignano cemetery must have frightened and confused survivors as the situation continued for a month or more in the high heat of July-August of circa 450 C.E.[5]

THE INFANT CEMETERY

A burial spot needed to be chosen quickly in which to inter the infants who had died and were continuing to die. A place that was otherwise unusable, i.e. the ruins of a villa that took up much of the large rather flat hilltop of Poggio Gramignano, could be tidied up and turned into a suitable burial ground for the untimely dead. An out of the way location was needed because the souls of dead infants were widely believed to be dangerous. This was because their full life-span was never reached and the life force of such children might be or might already have been harnessed for use in spells and potions or for the promotion of evil by demons or witches, as will be discussed below (see Footnote 71). Poggio Gramignano was probably at a considerable distance from the community of the living, although no concentrated settlement of the living has yet been found. In any case, the land occupied by a ruined villa was of little value because it could not be occupied and was unsuitable for agriculture as it could not be ploughed. Furthermore, burying infants within a space once inhabited by the living echoed earlier traditions further demonstrating the connection between the living community and their traditional beliefs and practices (see Footnote 7).

Some of the infant burials were entombed reusing roof tiles from the ruined villa to build simple interments known as *a coppa* (with terra cotta roof cover tiles; Figure 6), or tombs using primarily *tegulae* or roof tiles known as *alla capuccina* type (Figure 7), or still others built up of a mix of tile types to make small house-like tombs (Figure 8). In other cases transport amphorae or pieces of them, mostly from North Africa, were pressed into service as containers for the victims in a burial type known as *enchytrismos* (in ancient Greek, exposing or burying an infant within a jar or pot) (Figure 9). Many burials were simple inhumation type (Figure 10; Figure 11). Funerary offerings as we have seen ranged from non-existent to simple but were often of ritual significance.[6]

Of course death from *Plasmodium falciparum* malaria would also have resulted for adults but there are no adult burials in this cemetery and that cemetery has not yet been found, nor is it known if any children were buried in the adult cemetery. It may well be that the adult cemetery is not far away, perhaps less than a quarter mile further along the hilltop of Poggio Gramignano to the northwest among extensive ruins recently revealed by satellite imagery and which apparently pertain to the production area of the villa. These are discussed in our (at this time forthcoming) second volume.

Since literary sources, and even the rare depictions of children, portray elite status and social conformity, archaeological analysis of infant burials and their funerary ritual are our best chance at examining how women actually dealt with infant death and mourning. Before perhaps the later third or fourth centuries A.D. children who were not of sufficient age might be discarded or buried *suggrundaria* which might be taken to mean under the eaves literally or more generally around

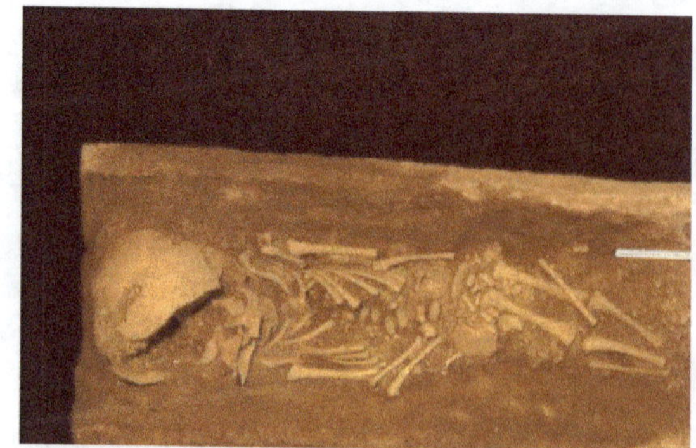

FIGURE 6 Burial 37 of Room 17 after removal of roof cover tile from over the burial and with cover tile remaining under the burial of the 9.5 lunar month child.

FIGURE 8 Burial 40 from Room 17 before opening, containing 2 infants aged birth to two months and four to six months. Tomb is of the House of Tiles type including seven pan tile fragments, three cover tile fragments, one dolium fragment and twenty stones.

FIGURE 7 Burial 39 of Room 17 of 4 to 6 month old infant. Tomb is of Capuchin Type shown prior to opening, featuring pan roof tiles and tile fragments placed to form a pyramid. The body inside was placed on two pan tiles.

FIGURE 9 Burial 1 from threshold Rooms 11 & 12, containing infant (rebult by Walter Birkby from the original bones) aged 10 lunar months inside partial *spatheion* amphora.

the home rather than in a formal graveyard. However, Maureen Carroll has found that although infants and children can appear in isolation from adult graves, they are more commonly interspersed in cemeteries with older children and adults.[7] Infants less than 1 year old appear in virtually all Roman era Italian cemeteries, yet the proportion of infants per cemetery is much lower than the estimated mortality rate of 20 to 30%.[8] Burial within their own distinct cemetery or within a separate part of the adult cemetery certainly was well established by the fifth century in Christian doctrine.[9]

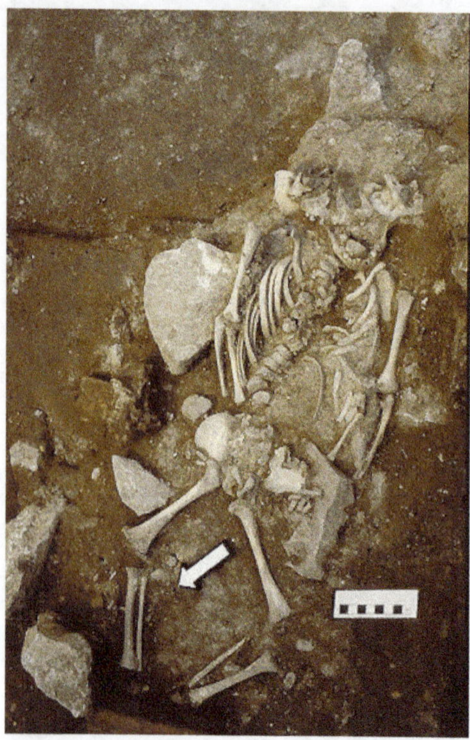

FIGURE 10 Simple inhumation Burial 36 of 2 to 3 year old infant found with its cranium (not shown) to the southeast and with small stone in its mouth. The body was weighed down with a cobble stone over the right hand and a 13cm long stone over the left hand. The feet were weighed down with a large pan tile and a square limestone.

FIGURE 11 Upper portion of skull from Burial 36 showing *cribra orbitalia* pitting on the upper area of the eye orbit.

In this rural area around A.D. 450 when Christianity was growing increasingly dominant in Italy a revival or revitalization of earlier practices including witchcraft, talismans and apotropaics occurred and tried to stem the perceived evil influences. The ancient community at Poggio Gramignano did not identify and understand diseases (e.g., malaria) in the same way we understand them today, through a biomedical lens, and they responded to it in their own manner and likely believed to have finally achieved the return of normalcy to the community. But what was actually occurring was likely the spread of an unknown disease which ran its course as the weather warmed and then finally cooled over several months, and which could have affected other communities along the Tiber. To them, it must have seemed as if their revitalization or nativistic movement, bringing back the old ways, was working. But what were the old ways and what were they afraid of?[10]

ROMAN ATTITUDE TO INFANT DEATH AND BURIAL

While scholars formerly asserted that the Romans were indifferent to infant death and mourning, it has become more and more clear in recent scholarship that this claim is not generally true. This belief stems primarily from various ancient literary sources, which prescribe differentiated mourning periods and/or burial practices depending on the age of the child, or which shame emotional responses to child death.[11] However, the commemoration of infants and children in cemeteries across Italy and the Roman provinces reflects an opposing reality. As shown by the work of Carroll, Norman, Wilson and others, the situation is much more complex.[12] Children and infants certainly seem to have been members of their communities and their deaths sources of grief. Yet there is also evidence that belief in the *mors immatura* (early death) and ritual actions taken in response were commonplace, particularly in response to stress from epidemic events, and they affected the treatment of dead children. These aspects of infant burial are relevant to our study of the infant cemetery at Poggio Gramignano (Lugnano in Teverina).

As pointed out by Wilson, the literary sources referenced by scholars for parental detachment in the ancient world were produced by an elite male fraction of the population.[13] This neglects the perspective of women and rural non-elites, who presumably would comprise the majority of the population who would be using the cemetery at Poggio Gramignano. Nonetheless, various Roman authors establish a marginal position for infants and children in Roman society. For example, Plutarch, Cicero, Paulus, and Ulpian indicate non-existent or restrained levels of mourning depending on the age of the child.[14] Juvenal and Pliny remark that children who have not reached teething age are too young to be cremated on the funeral pyre.[15] There are also indications that infants were considered to be "non-persons", with comparisons of infants to plants or the idea that they lacked a soul.[16] On the other hand, we also find a fragmentary reflection of the experience of women in these sources. Plutarch claims that Roman mothers experienced maddened grief from the death of children, and several sources shame men for grieving like women. However, Plutarch also expresses his own grief for their daughter in this text, and his main point does not seem to be that they should not mourn their daughter, but that they should, "cherish her memory, which will conduce many ways—or rather many fold— more to (their) joy than (their) grief," and they should mourn in relative privacy.[17] Sympathetic depictions of infant death in myth, like that of Opheltes in Statius' *Thebaid* or of the touchingly wailing, prematurely dead infant spirits in Virgil's *Aeneid* also confirm that the notion that Romans were apathetic towards child death is simplistic and not always true.[18]

The example from the *Aeneid* also brings up the idea of the *mors immatura*, and was cited by Émile Jobbé-Duval over a century ago when he noted that infants and others who die prematurely present a threat to the living.[19] This category of dangerous dead might warrant non-normative burial ritual like positioning or weighing down of the body to prevent the rise of the dead or including apotropaic grave goods. However, not only were these ritual actions meant to protect the living from the immaturely dead, but they were also intended to protect the dead from witchcraft and to help them rest peacefully. This also shows a level of care and respect for the young deceased.

Clearly the archaeological evidence shows that some percentage of infants were not formally buried, which may be due to the status or wealth of the parents. Pliny's remarks on the practice of inhuming younger infants holds true in most Roman Italian cemeteries, but there are exceptions at Porta Nocera, and sites in Gaul where infants were cremated.[20] Both infants and children are commonly buried with grave goods, which range from childhood items like feeding bottles to generic items like lamps or coins. Occasionally, measures to ward off witchcraft or appease the *mors immatura* appear, such as apotropaic amulets or symbolic items like a nail meant to 'nail' down the spirit of the dead are found.[21] However, only children over a year old seem to be buried with more prestigious items.

The care in the placing of the bodies, the integration of infant burials into cemeteries, and the presence of grave goods all indicate that infants were mourned and had some social identity. This contradicts the literary evidence which was previously taken at face value by classical archaeologists. The typical circumstances surrounding infant and child burial which Carroll establishes have allowed us to better analyze the abnormalities of the Lugnano cemetery. The absence of adults from the cemetery, the increasing frequency of depositions, and the presence of both normative and non-normative burial positioning all present a unique case thus far in late antique Roman archaeology and have merited special treatment archaeologically for our cemetery.

ATYPICAL FINDS FROM THE INFANT CEMETERY

When the University of Arizona was invited in 1987 by the local Comune of Lugnano in Teverina, their Associazione Pro-Loco and the Soprintendenza per l'Umbria to investigate the ruins of Poggio Gramignano, it was only known to be the site of a Roman villa. Preliminary excavation, however, through the backfill of probes made by a previous excavator revealed the presence of fragments of two apparent neo-nates and suggested that more burials might be present. At that point, implementation of a micro-stratigraphic approach including excavating with the presence of several forensic anthropologists, a palynologist and a stratigraphic analyst was employed. This effort was rewarded when actual burials and evidence of a significant infant cemetery were found. Because the delicacy of scattered or rodent-dragged infant bones and the settling of burials filled in with lightly compacted soil had to be considered, extensive fine mesh sieving was employed which led to the recovery of unusual and delicate finds from the multiple burials.[22]

In addition to the complete burials of the infants, numerous objects were found as a result of the employed methodology which suggested the use of magic and apotropaic rituals within the burial area. Not all of the interments had offerings or were buried with any elaboration, suggesting varying degrees of mourning, fear and/or poverty by the families, and one must also consider that such conclusions must be judged preliminary because many perishable offerings have left no discernible trace in the archaeological record. The following paragraphs present the burials where key finds were able to have been recovered from the cemetery, which impacted our consideration of what occurred here.

Infant burials (IBs) 8a and 8b were possible twins aged 9.5 to 10 lunar months who were found in Room 11 along with the internal manual phalanx of a third individual (possibly the distal portion of a thumb), aged shortly pre-teen to early teens[23] (Figure 12). The wear and subtle sun bleaching on the element, along with the absence of other skeletal remains from an appropriately aged individual nearby (such as Burial 51), suggests it could have been gathered from another location, possibly another cemetery where it had been exposed to the elements, and finally placed as an offering here.

A human bone, easily gathered from the surface of another cemetery, is the sort of object one would expect to have been valued by a necromancer, in this case perhaps someone like a *goes*, originally γόης, a Greek word meaning someone who literally howls out enchantments or engages in sorcery and who might be charged with protecting the community. His (or her?) work may also be involved with mourning the loss of someone, as it is derived from the Greek verb γοάω which suggests groaning, moaning and weeping. He would also be someone involved with calming or appeasing or

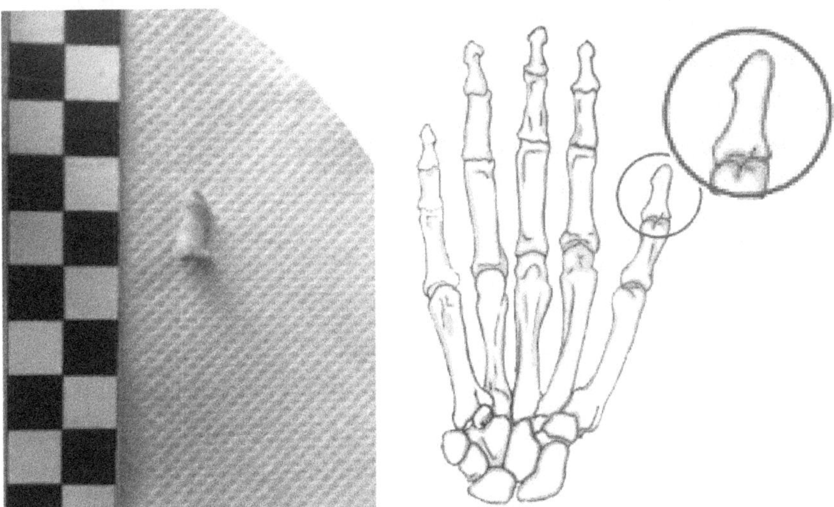

FIGURE 12 Manual phalanx (digital hand bone) found with a double burial 8a and 8b of infants of 9.5 to 10 lunar months from Room 11, possible twins.

even facilitating conversation with the restless dead and he could be an esteemed member of a local community performing an acknowledged and respected function, assuaging and keeping the dead in check through magical formulae and special rites.[24]

In Room 11, a raven's talon was found placed directly on the body of Infant Burial 3, an infant of 8 to 8.5 lunar months, above which was found a tiny copper alloy bracelet for a child[25] (Figure 13). The raven talon brings to mind images of bird talons or claws used by witches and a *strix* and is associated with a terrifying revenant child, as will be discussed below in Horace's *Epode* V and Ovid's *Fasti* VI. It also recalls the talon feet of the bird demon Lilith about which more will also be said. Bird demons with sharp talons were thought to come and snatch babies from their mother and this offering together with a "knucklebone" (sheep *astragalus* or ankle bone) found just below the burial may have been intended to function as a talisman. On numerous sites, particularly in England, raven burials have been found from the Iron Age into the Roman Period, particularly in association with puppies,[26] al-

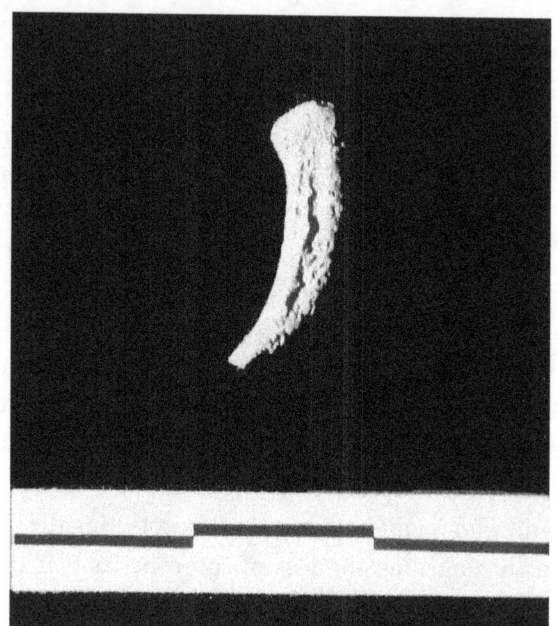

FIGURE 13 Raven's talon found with a fetus of 8 to 8.5 lunar months in Room 11.

though the precise reason for the offerings is not yet known. It has been suggested that the ravens' ability to "talk", their great size, adoptability as pets, their traditional role as prophets of doom and even their alleged abilities as shape-shifters, as well as their color make them possible liminal links between the otherworld beyond the grave and the world of the living. Furthermore, the talon is the symbol, bar none, of the claw of the child-snatching demon bird. The practice of raven sacrifice is particularly prominent in England in the Roman period.[27] Sarah Iles Johnston has pointed out in a personal communication that ravens "are primarily carrion eaters, not birds of prey (although they will sometimes attack baby animals or sick animals)" and this, along with their other more human-friendly pet-like characteristics and their dark other-worldly appearance may help to promote them as acceptable links between the living and the dead and intercessors for the deceased.

IBs 20a and b in Room 15, 9.5 to 10 lunar months, are believed to be twins and were buried with a copper alloy finger ring just southeast of 20a. Another finger ring was found by the knee of IB 22

(8.5 to 9.5 lunar months) in Room 17, while a piece of iron slag had been apparently placed on the body of IB 21, which was aged 8 to 8.5 lunar months in Room 15. IBs 15 and 17 in Room 10 were neonate to one week in age with IB 15 being placed under a reused roof cover tile. Both were in close proximity to a puppy and an immature dog.

Directly on IB 33, aged 6 lunar months to 2 weeks and found in Room 11, was a small toad (*bufo*) which was an offering or pet burial[28] (Fig. 14). Directly under that burial was placed a single knucklebone (*astragalus*), which might simply represent a popular children's game but numerous examples of knucklebones from tombs of various periods and sites in Italy are known and are sometimes arranged in apotropaic patterns around the dead. It is thought that the frequency of these and especially their use in children's tombs suggest that they were not only gaming pieces associated with children but also used to protect the living from the spirits of the dead.[29]

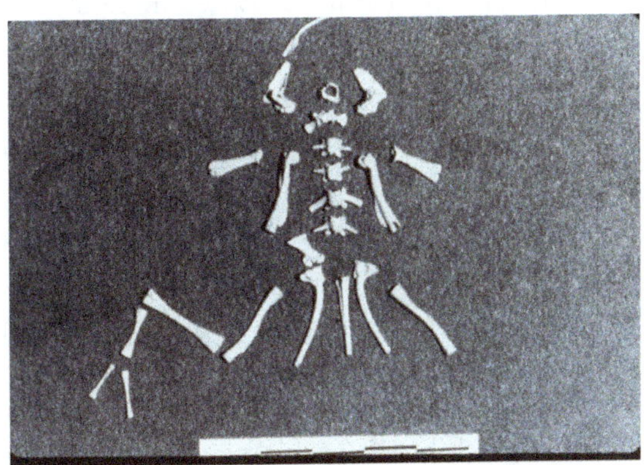

FIGURE 14 Small toad found resting on infant burial 33 of 6 lunar months to two weeks of age in Room 11.

A fragmentary bone doll was found in the threshold between Rooms 11 and 12 on IB 6, 5 to 6 months of age[30] (Figure 15). The doll had summarily indicated facial features, a navel and pubic area, and had a tang but no legs (they were probably separately added) and no preserved arms, although the projected stubs may have been intended to indicate breasts. It had been placed against the burial and there was ash deposited on the body which revealed traces of burnt *ulmus* (elm tree), *olea* (olive tree), *quercus ilex* (evergreen oak) and 3 traces of *spartium* (rush or weaver's broom, a shrub with yellow flowers).

Additional finds recovered included a large scattering of honeysuckle (*Lonicera caprifolium*), an unusual offering but which was known in antiquity as a cure or aid for splenomegaly, according to Pliny the Elder.[31] It is known as Italian woodbine which blooms ca. mid July with beautiful and fragrant flowers:

FIGURE 15 Fragmentary bone doll found in the threshold between Rooms 11 and 12 and on infant burial 6, aged 5 to 6 months.

nascitur in arvis ac saepibus circumvolvens se adminiculis quibuscumque…hi resoluti dantur in vini albi cyathis ternis tricenis diebus ad lienem, eumque urina cruentata aut per alvum absumit, quod intellegitur a decimo statim die.

The plant grows in cultivated fields and in hedges, climbing round supports of any kind. These [seeds], dissolved in three cyathi of white wine, are given for thirty days to cure splenic affections, the spleen being reduced either by blood in the urine or through the bowels, as is plain immediately from the tenth day.

Among the other offerings discovered during the excavation was one upside-down cooking pot, two complete bronze cauldrons placed upright one inside the other, 3 late antique small copper alloy coins, and 3 iron nails which were either offerings or simply part of the villa debris.

The bronze cauldrons[32] (Figure 16 and Figure 17) were found in Room 12 in soft soil 20cm below and just north of IB 4, which itself had been found in a *spatheion* amphora and was estimated to be 4.5 to 5.5 months in age. The cauldrons showed significant traces of burning of wood including *Olea* inside, *Ulmus* and *Quercus cerris* (Turkey or Austrian oak) on the upper cauldron rim and more *Quercus cerris* and *Olea* in the surrounding area along with *Quercus ilex* (evergreen oak). Just southeast of the amphora was found an illegible late Roman period copper alloy coin. In fact, not only the cauldrons and their area but the entire cemetery was filled with significant lenses of ashy soil which held evidence of *spartium*, *cypressus/juniperus* (juniper), and *rosaceae* (the rose family). *Spartium* was easily gathered in the villa area and good to use for small fires but the use of roses may have coincided with the *Rosalia* festival, celebrated in summer from later May through mid July, wherein it was customary to place roses at the graves of the dead.

Three large complete iron nails were found scattered within the cemetery. There were 29 incomplete nails found belonging to several basic Roman carpentry types but only one was found directly connected with an infant burial, placed directly over IBs 14 and 24. This double burial had been made by placing an amphora burial inside a fragmentary *spatheion* amphora (from Africa and featuring a long narrow body) which also contained a burial. The infants were 9 to 9.5 lunar months in age. This type of iron nail was normally used for general carpentry.[33] Numerous articles have been published citing the inclusion of large iron nails as *defixiones* to keep the dead in their place and protect the living and Pliny the Elder has noted several times that iron has the power when employed in certain rituals to resist magic.[34] It may even be that the iron slag fragment placed apparently deliberately on IBs 8a and 8b discussed above was intended to have the same function.

FIGURE 16 Two bronze cauldrons found placed one inside the other in Room 12.

FIGURE 17 One of the bronze cauldrons found in Room 12 after cleaning and restoration.

The upside-down cooking pot was associated in Room 17 with IB 40 which was two infants (neonate to 2 months and 4 to 6 months in age) interred in a Double Capuchin tomb (Figure 18 and Figure 19). The pot had no base but apparently had been inverted as an offering to chthonic deities and contained inside it a rib and unidentified scraps of mammal bones, as well as a badly preserved and shattered small glass pouring vessel (*anforetta*) of the late fourth to the fifth century.[35] The mouth and part of the handle remain. The rim is folded back externally to form a sort of collar. The handle joins at the rim, and originally went down vertically to secure itself on the shoulder. Traces of *Lonicera caprifolium* were found all around the cooking pot suggesting that it was part of the offering ritual in addition to the other items that were burned. Closely associated with IB 40 was a large quantity of *Quercus cerris*, *Olea europea*, and *Quercus ilex*. Also found within the upside-down pot itself were charred remains of *Olea*, *Quercus cerris*, *Quercus ilex* and several scraps of indeterminate worked bone.   IB 48, about 7 lunar months, was also found in Room 17 and had 2 upside-down cooking pots buried next to it along with a metal ring and a poorly preserved late Roman copper alloy coin.[36]

FIGURE 18 Upside-down cooking ware pot found in Room 17, as found.

Finally, associated with numerous burials and scattered throughout the cemetery were found burnt traces of *Rhamnus alaternus*, which is the shrub buckthorn. It was found particularly on a threshold block between Rooms 11 and 12 along with traces of bone from an unidentified animal, perhaps intended as an offering to Hecate as a goddess of thresholds. The shrub burns with a foul odor and during the *Anthesteria* festival celebrating the beginning of spring in ancient Athens. Honoring Dionysus, people chewed it because it was thought to be able to keep away ghosts. It was thought that during the festival period dead souls could emerge from the underworld and walk about. In addition the *rhamnus* plant was hung on house doors for

FIGURE 19 Upside-down cooking pot from Room 17.

protection against *daimones* or evil forces when women were giving birth, since there were believed to be ghosts and demons that specialized in killing infants and pregnant women.[37]

In addition to the above-mentioned finds were numerous pigs (*Sus scrofa*), comprising 59.8% of all the animal bones found in the infant cemetery and 48% of those were younger than 1.5 years. There were abundant butchering marks showing that piglets were perhaps a ritual meal of choice here and one is reminded of the passage in Ovid's *Fasti* of the use of the gutted innards of a two-month-old female pig or sow to help prevent an infant-snatching demon called a *strix* from doing the same thing to five-day-old little Proca and no doubt to other children in the future.[38] Chickens and chicken eggshells were also found in significant quantities suggesting that they too were consumed avidly here.[39]

DOG BURIALS

In addition to the finds already cited within the infant cemetery, the presence of sacrificed dogs was another indicator of the need for guardians and protectors of the dead. In all, a total of 13 dogs were found amid the infant burials in Rooms 10, 11, 12 and 15 of the villa. 12 of them were puppies estimated to range from 2 weeks to 4 to 6 months in age and 1 was an immature dog estimated at 1 year to 14 months in age.[40] Puppies 1 to 3 were found in Room 10, puppies 4 to 10 in Rooms 11 and 12 which were adjoining rooms, puppies 11 and 12 were found in Room 15 and the immature dog in Room 10. Puppy number 10 was able to be dated more specifically to 6 or up to 7 months in age. No traces of cut marks for butchery were found on the dog remains and all dogs appeared to be healthy although some evidence suggested they may have been skinned. As paleo-osteologist Michael McKinnon has stated:

> "The relative lack of metacarpal, metatarsal, and phalanx1 bones coupled with the complete absence of phalanx 2 and 3 bones may suggest that the puppies were skinned. These elements are within the paws of the dog, and may have been discarded with the skin. A careful or skilled individual may have been able to remove the skin and leave the metapodials and first phalanges perhaps, while a hasty individual may simply have ripped the skin, possibly taking whole paws with it. However, all of these bones are very small, and may have simply disintegrated in the soil, or fallen through the screens during sieving."[41]

Puppies 1, 4, 6 and 12 were fairly complete, while puppy 5 was represented only by the head. Puppies 2,3,9 and 11 were mostly complete but lacked mandibles which showed evidence of possibly having been literally ripped away. Puppies 7, 8 and 10 and the immature dog had mandibles and bodies but no head. Perhaps most bizarre of all was puppy number 10 which appeared to have been severed in two at the stomach (Figure 20). The two halves were buried a little over a meter apart with one part being the lower limbs and left mandible and no skull was found. The suggestion was made by zooarchaeologist Michael MacKinnon that not enough puppies could be found to bury with all the dead infants and so some pieces of puppy were buried with or near other infants in these rooms, the purpose being to somehow spread out the protective qualities of the dogs.

One complete puppy was found in Room 10 by IB 17 which was believed to be a double

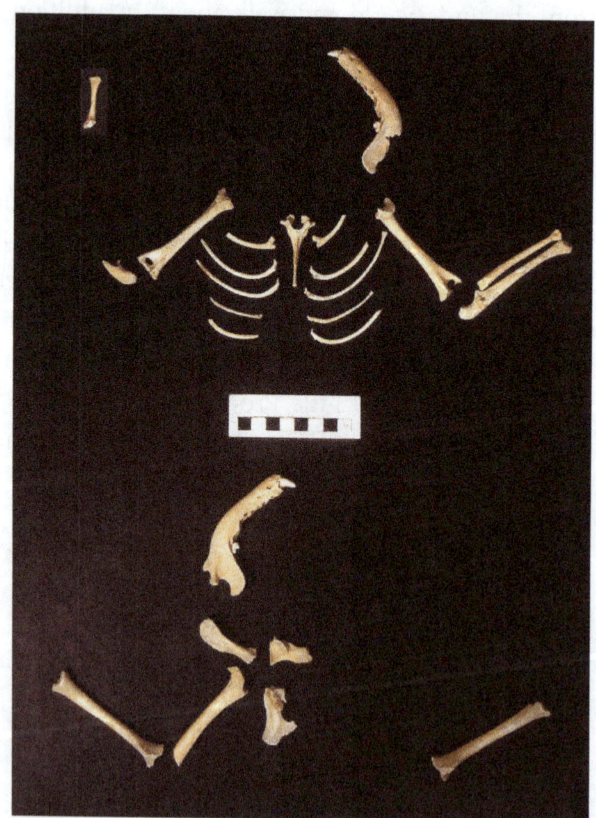

FIGURE 20 Puppy Number 10 was found split into two parts across the middle.

burial with IB 15. Both of the infants were neonates. One fragment of an immature dog was also found here. In one case, along with 15 pieces of charred *Quercus ilex* (holly oak) and a small quantity of *Cupressus/Juniperus* (juniper) and *Rosaceae* (roses), a tile reused from the ruins of the Roman villa on this site was pressed into use with IB 23 in Room 15 (10 lunar months to neonate) immediately to the southwest of the burial. Likely it was selected because it contained the imprint of a dog paw on it, made while the tile was originally still wet and drying. Unfortunately the faint print would only give information about the dog who was alive when the villa tile was made, likely in the 30s B.C., and would not be relevant to the sacrificed dogs of the fifth century A.D.

Dog dismemberment is attested in numerous sites in Europe and the Mediterranean including examples from Switzerland and Sardis.[42] The lack of exposure of any of the dog bones and the placement of them at various levels in soft earth supports the notion that the entire cemetery was installed over a short period of time. The dogs were placed within the burial areas of the various rooms, except for Room 17, but for the most part separately interred and placed at a short distance from the infant burials.

MacKinnon has postulated that the dogs may have been mastiffs which were short-muzzled and were known to have been bred in Umbria. They had excellent scenting abilities and so were valued hunting dogs and guard dogs and were used in agricultural areas with shepherds.[43]

Dogs had many different functions in Roman society and in the ancient world in general, which may explain the inclusion of puppies in the child cemetery of Poggio Gramignano. Aside from their position as beloved pets or working animals, they also appeared frequently in ritual contexts, both funerary and religious, as early as the Neolithic period in Italy and throughout Europe.[44]

Dogs are the best-documented companion animals of the Roman world, with references in letters, literature, and many epitaphs. As tame animals, they functioned primarily both as hunting dogs and as pets.[45] Dogs might also find occupations as guards, like those discussed by Columella in the mid first century A.D.[46] For example, Pliny the Elder discusses the intelligence and usefulness of dogs for the hunt, and even attests to a dog of Alexander the Great taking down lions and elephants.[47] Xenophon of Athens wrote extensively of the use of hounds in hunting in his fourth century B.C. *Cynegeticus* and Arrian later expanded on this with a personal account of his favorite dog. Not only does he discuss the dogs' ideal hunting qualities, but Xenophon also emphasizes the animals' devotion and affectionate personality.[48] Thus, his dog Horme acted both as a hunting hound and daily companion. Of course, the companionship role of dogs is also clear from various heartrending epitaphs and depictions of puppies and mature dogs in funerary reliefs.[49] These epitaphs exist for lap dogs and hunting dogs alike, extolling their virtues and their too-short lives.

Archaeological evidence clearly shows the special place that dogs occupied in the Roman family. For example, a toy-breed sized dog buried with an adolescent in the Yasmina cemetery shows signs of advanced periodontal disease and arthritis, ante-mortem. The care in the placement of the body and the advancement of these diseases prior to its death suggest that the dog received special attention and care from its owners throughout its relatively long illness.[50]

The ritual use of dogs dates further back than even the Romans understood. For example, the disarticulated bones of dogs, with signs of ritual butchering were found in Neolithic context in Continenza Cave in the Abruzzo area of north central Italy near the remains of humans.[51]

One of the most famous examples of the presumably ritual use of dogs may be the The Agora Bone Well wherein some 460 humans, mostly newborn or very young infants, and 150 intentionally selected mostly mature dogs were found in a well near the Athenian agora and apparently deposited between 180 and 150 B.C. It is possible that such combinations of infants and dogs may relate particularly to the association of dogs with birth goddesses such as Eileithyia and Genetyllis and others in connection with Hecate.[52] It may be that the reason for the ritual of the puppies found in Poggio Gramignano also had ancient origins, which may have been deeply ingrained in the community there and/or was passed on to them from other cultures and areas.

Recent discoveries (such as those at Peltuinum to be discussed presently) suggest that dogs were traditional protectors of the dead, especially children, as appears to also be supported by the Poggio Gramignano cemetery. They also looked after the house and particularly the household threshold where it was not uncommon to find the term "*cave canem* or "beware of the dog" at the entry, as in the case of the House of the Tragic Poet at Pompeii.[53]

But as Alessio Sassù has noted:

> "Dogs appear as ambiguous animals, characterised by different kinds of behaviour and by a double nature. They are the master's loyal attendants, a child's playing companions, but they can become aggressive when they are called upon to be the guardians of the household, or become monstrous when they are associated with Hecate's frightening escort."[54]

Sassù also points out that in antiquity dogs were never pure enough to be sacrificed to the Olympian gods. Dog sacrifices to divinities such as Hecate, according to Sassù, were often made to avert and expiate evil. This mixture of pure and impure nature for the dog was also noted by Plutarch.[55]

STONES/TILES PLACED IN THE MOUTHS OR OVER THE BODIES OF DEAD CHILDREN

Among the most bizarre characteristics of the burials on the hilltop at Poggio Gramignano is the presence of stones placed over the bodies and in the mouths of older children such as Infant Burial 36 (a toddler two to three years of age) and Infant Burial 51 (a child 8 to 12 years old). IB 36 had the wrists weighed down with stones and a heavy stone and roof tile placed over the ankles and feet apparently to keep the dead child from rising[56] (Figure 10; Figure 11). This was the same individual who tested positively for *Plasmodium falciparum* malaria by Sallares and Gomzl in 2001 and it was found adjacent to Infant Burial 59, aged 9 months to 1 year, which had been placed within fragments of an amphora. Infant Burial 51 was made in *a cappuccina* style. In addition, Infant Burial 49 of 6.5 to 7 lunar months had a tile placed over the body in Room 17.

Infant Burial 51 (Figure 21; Figure 22; Figure 23), 8 to 12 years and the oldest child yet recovered, was found in Room 17 buried *a cappuccina* style and not only had a limestone placed in its mouth but was buried with two small beads, a copper alloy candelabrum fragment (Figure 24), an iron pickaxe head or *dolabra* (Figure 25), a possible color mixing palette stone which appears to be made of slate, not native to this area, and a cow skull[57] (Figure 26). Infant Burial 57, 0 to 2 months, also was found with a small stone in its mouth while Infant Burial 55 of the same age was found with a large stone placed over the body and showing evidence of perhaps wearing a shroud or swaddling clothes. Romans used *dolabrae* such as this to slaughter large animals—so it may be associated with the cow skull and candelabrum and be a ritual performed at night.[58]

The overall impression one might take away from the unusual offerings and treatment of the infants is that there was a definite concern that these babies were somehow contaminated not only with disease but with a pollutant that had taken possession of their souls, and that they

FIGURE 21 Infant Burial 51 from Room 17, aged 8 to 12 years, after removal of several covering tiles.

FIGURE 22 Detail of Infant Burial 51 showing the stone placed in the mouth of the child

FIGURE 23 Limestone after removal from the mouth of the child.

FIGURE 24 Fragmentary copper alloy lampstand as found

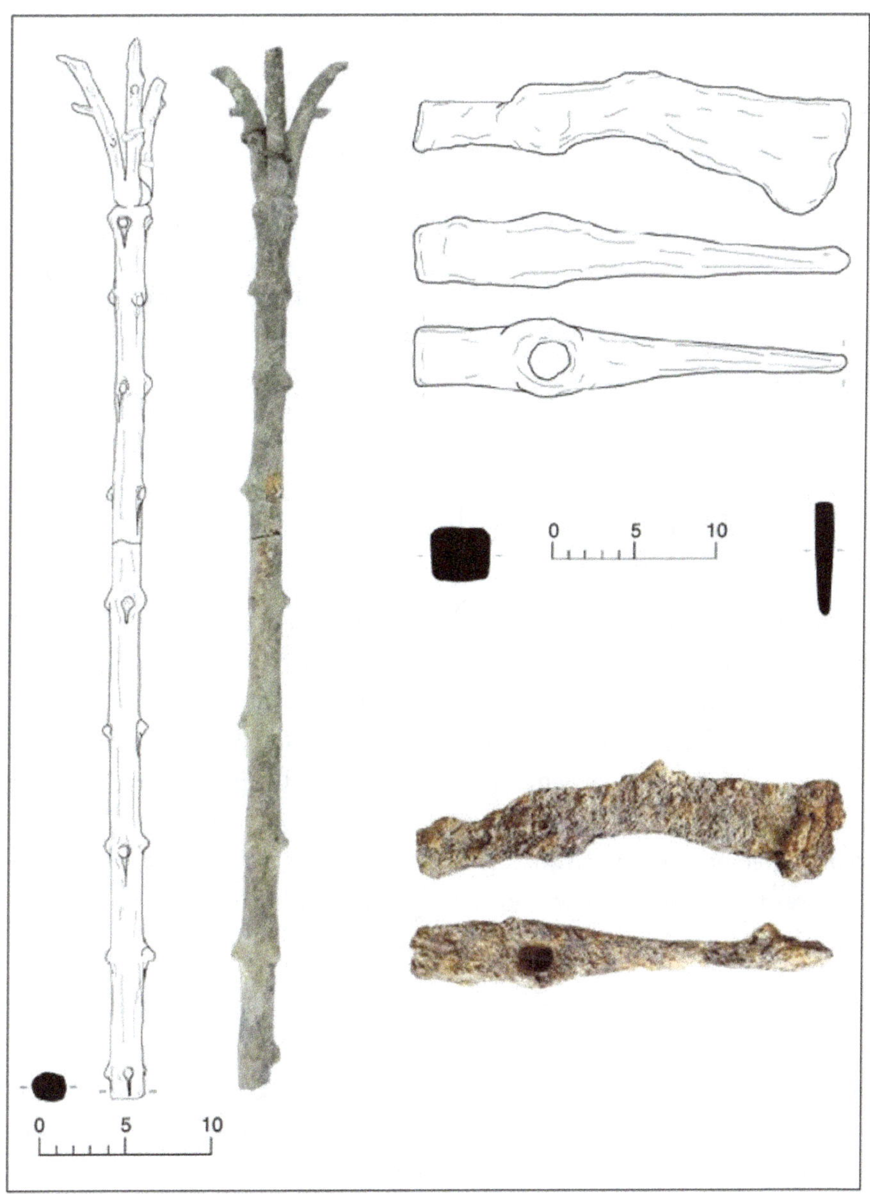

Fig. 5. A sinistra, portalucerna in bronzo; a destra, testa d'ascia in ferro (foto M. Elefante, S. Jenkins).

FIGURE 25 Lampstand fragment compared to a complete parallel lampstand, and the *dolabra* or pickaxe found near Infant Burial 51.

needed talismans and rituals of various sorts to both protect them and at the same time keep their spirits from being harnessed by evil forces that might compel them to rise from the dead and spread horror among the living as revenants. It seems that babies and infants whose lives were never fulfilled and who had died prematurely were thought of as potentially dangerous since their unfulfilled nature might be harnessed by demons or witches with evil intent. At the very least it is clear that Roman demons showed an uncommon fondness for abducting, terrifying and/or killing fetuses and babies.[59]

It is also possible that the physical appearance of these children as malaria ravaged them would have contributed to the anxiety of the parents and general community. Victims would have become pale and wan, convulsing with the fever as though being manipulated by some malevolent force[60] (Figure 11).

WHO WAS IN CHARGE OF THE BURIALS?

Another major question about the site is who was taking charge of the situation of escalating infant deaths. Was it a physician, individual families, or a community leader, particularly a spiritual leader? Because the delivery of the infants was likely assisted by a midwife, such an individual (or individuals) may have been involved in attempts to save the children and mother. A logical extension of this is to assume she might also be knowledgeable about burying the potentially "polluting" or "dangerous" dead, even the very small. The midwife might also be responsible for taking care of the mother even after a baby died or a fetus were miscarried but how did a midwife respond to a pandemic such as this? What was the midwife's full responsibility at this moment and what is the evidence at the cemetery for midwife birthing?

Of particular note is that Hecate was a goddess to whom one could pray for overall protection, from whom one could ask for favorable spells, apotropaic amulets and advice to avert evil or to protect babies. Midwives (*obstetrices*) were birthing specialists whose knowledge of the dangerous, fragile act of childbirth might also include sometimes the function of a *saga* or prophetess/interpreter of signs. As such they might determine what purifying spells to use, what amulets the mother should wear, plus interpretations of the divine and the mystical, drawing on their own years of experience and success rate at delivering and caring for infants and mothers.[61]

Pliny the Elder gives a whole list of what might be called folk remedies that can be employed supposedly effectively but of course these are not accepted in modern medical standards and practices. Midwives of quality were often trained in or came from the Greek east where the profession had a more elevated level (they even might publish treatises!) and in Rome the finest midwives might be attached to the wealthiest and most important families who seem to have been able to have their own medical care, much in the fashion of today's private personal doctors who can be on call at any time for the wealthy if an annual fee is paid. The *sagae* of our cemetery were likely to be local women and not eastern medical experts or the sort of women with a medical reputation who attended high families. They were likely simply members of the community with that community's skill set and religious beliefs.[62]

As further evidence of the variation in quality and perceived function of midwifery, Soranus, writing in the 2nd century A.D., had to advise midwives not to be superstitious because apparently spells and witchcraft were sometimes used too much by them and he counseled that they generally should be well read![63] A midwife might be expected to know what liturgical lamentations and expressions were appropriate and useful, the so-called *devotiones sepularales* or death spells appropriate for graveyards and funerals since childbirth often led to death.

But what variation in feeling there was about such devotions is difficult to assess without more help from ancient texts on the subject. It is not known exactly what role a religious leader in the community would carry in a situation where something bizarre has occurred or what exactly he (or she?) might be called. Would the community turn to what in Greek would be termed the γόης (in Latin the *goes*) rather than a μάγος or *magus*. The latter had connotations of magic, sorcery and even the ability to shape-shift but also carried pejorative connotations at times, associated with quackery. A *saga* or wise woman might also be called upon but might have alleged powers that were perceived as magic-based. A γόης however might be thought of as specializing in contacting the souls of the dead to expiate a plague or disaster within a community. A *magus* might originally have been a Chaldean priest-king or eastern sorcerer/astrologer but by the mid fifth century A.D. the term seems to have grown in popular usage but also in widespread disapproval which had begun even in the early Empire.[64]

PARALLELS

Nothing quite like the bizarre events at Poggio Gramignano has been found at other sites in Italy, although one excavation has yielded some possible parallels. The Roman site of Peltuinum in the Abruzzi has some similarities.[65] Unlike the Poggio Gramignano situation, however, the time span of the Peltuinum burials is less clear. The excavation revealed the filling up of pits that were originally dug inside a theater with infant burials and dogs along with a small number of cats and foals. The dogs, which appear to have been ritually slaughtered, were placed atop the pits and were interpreted as being intended to be guardians of the infants. The excavators interpreted the find as exhibiting normal infant mortality rates, although the unusual burials could have been the result of an epidemic or disaster of some kind. One is certainly left to wonder why there are so many unusual offerings accompanying the discarded infants. It is as if the locals themselves at the time were finding their high infant death rate surprising and even frightening? However, apart from the included animals no evidence of magic rites or apotropaics was recovered in, on or around the burials.

In Gubbio, just 100 miles due north of Poggio Gramignano in Umbria, the so-called Iguvine Tablets of the third to first centuries B.C. mention dog sacrifices to Jupiter. These tablets prescribed elaborate religious sacrificial rites involving puppies and a wide variety of other available animals practiced as apotropaics against evil and the tablets also contain formulae for offerings to cause harm to enemies and appease divinities of the underworld.[66]

FEAR OF THE UNKNOWN AND UNEXPLAINED

Based on the information recovered thus far from the excavation and investigation into what the Romans themselves have noted in their literature about their own feelings, it appears evident that beneath the surface veneer of an orderly cosmos ruled by the major traditional divinities of the Romans in an age where Christianity had supposedly won the empire, there was a panoply of what might be termed folk divinities and demons who could protect a person or a community or bring it terror and death and these beliefs were more widespread than are commonly realized. Yet even today belief in what many perceive as established scientific fact is disputed by almost half of the population in the United States which believes in the supernatural.[67]

The Romans had many divinities who looked after the hazards of every aspect of birth which especially at this time in rural communities was considered enormously risky for women and even in major centers of living resulted in the deaths of the wives of numerous prominent individuals who had access to the best of care in their time.[68] Add to this some strange phenomenon at Poggio Gramignano that was producing still births and miscarried fetuses within a community and which was increasing daily in frequency and it is easy to see how mass hysteria would take over and unscientific and even unreasonable fear would trigger the need for specialized religious and community leaders conversant with the old ways which included a generous helping of what we would call witchcraft and help from those who understood how to perform the appropriate rituals. Also required would be action to isolate the affected and seemingly dangerous dying or already deceased children (and adults) from the surviving terrified community.

The babies were not found buried with adults and there seems to be very little if any separation by age or hierarchy within the cemetery. Some burials were rudimentary and had almost no offerings or attempt at a significant burial while others did, although all of the attempts at creating tombs were rudimentary and primarily done with reused material from the original villa and all of the offerings were of poor quality. The appearance to the excavators was of burials made in haste in a series of ruined rooms along the western part of the villa which afforded a convenient spot to hold some sort of service and to inter children, at first singly but as the conditions warranted, in pairs and finally small groups, filling in the earth around the bodies with ashy soil from the offerings made here. Rooms 11, 12 and 17 had been barrel vaulted but the vaults had partially fallen by the fifth century when the villa had long been out of use and there may have been a need to further break down the surviving vaulting in order to avoid a risk of it collapsing onto the cemetery-makers.

In each of the rooms were found fetuses and perinates, those babies less than a year in age and in Room 17 were found the two eldest children, a 2-3 year old and a 10-12 year old. In terms of burial types generally those with offerings and those without and all ranges of age could be found in each of the rooms. Puppies were not found buried in Room 17. Joins in pottery were found in both the old and new excavations from low to high levels, continuing to suggest that a very limited time elapsed in the construction of the cemetery. The rooms in which the infants were interred were themselves already partly filled up with creep and slump from the hillside immediately above them, due to the effect of heavy rains over several centuries since the villa ceased to function completely perhaps in the third century.

LITERARY PARALLELS FOR THE CEMETERY RITUALS

Considering the finds in this infant cemetery, the parallels which exist with the poetry of Horace and Virgil (and other Greek and Roman authors) are striking and suggest that fear of a demon or demons was palpable and magic may have been employed in our cemetery to protect the dead and also to protect the living from the dead.[69] The offerings represent a desire to lament the loss of a family member to varying degrees while at the same time the bereaved families apparently faced a constant fear from what had happened already to their community and what could potentially happen after the deceased has crossed over from the living to the dead or even potentially became living dead.

Cemeteries in Roman antiquity were both places to revere and lament the dead but also eerie places where one could observe the crossing of the threshold (*limen*) between life and death at which point all direct communication with the loved one ceased. There were various divinities and demons which could inhabit the Roman mind about this transitional space and a widespread belief in the ability of witches or necromancers to achieve control of this "space". Gravesites, especially sites such as this one, were marginalized. Yet in more normal cemeteries, especially in Greece, one had funnels that might enter below the surface to allow libations to be poured that were imagined to reach the deceased below with wine, milk, honey or other offerings.[70] Infants especially, when dead before their normal life span, were often considered contaminated and even an object of fear due to appropriation of their souls by a witch or demon, not to mention the possibility of a stigma against the unfortunate mother for failure to produce a healthy child, if she in fact lived through the experience.[71]

A MODERN PARALLEL

It is not easy to understand how the Romans in Rome and/or in the countryside viewed witches and demon spirits but a look at Horace particularly reveals that Romans could view witches both as comic figures and frightening agents of genuine horror simultaneously and it would seem hard for a modern mind to understand this concept. However, even in today's America television programs are full of pseudo-documentaries that celebrate so-called genuine "Ghost Hunters" in a genre described on Wikipedia as "paranormal reality programming".

Nonetheless, it is still hard for us to fully understand the credulity of a population faced with the unknown and the frightening. The author however can report first-hand about such matters, having spent 1974 to 1976 mostly in Thurburbo Maius in north central Tunisia and for 10 years working among Bedouins / Berbers there and at El Jem and Salakta in the foothills of the Sahara Desert. It was widely believed in the small community of Utique (ancient Utica in northeast Tunisia) in 1970 that a teenage girl belonging to one small Berber community had been given a love potion baked into a cake by the mother of a handsome boy in another small town. The possessed girl professed a powerful love for the boy and the parents were determined to break off the affair by using witchcraft. It was decided to see a shaman or male necromancer, a regional *altabib*, in fact the equivalent of a *γόης* in the witchcraft center of El Fahs, near the ancient Roman site of Thuburbo Maius and David Soren, having the only car, became the driver of the young girl and her mother and father to the *altabib's* home, a simple house among others along a back road.

A ceremony was held in semi-darkness with incantations of all sorts. Women attendants were present to look after the 15 year old. They were, Dr. Soren was told, middle aged and even older women who looked after other women young and old and followed the leader of the religious healing group, so that they were for all intents and purposes midwives in the fullest expansion of the term. The young lady was forced to swallow a piece of what appeared to be hamburger or ground horse meat which had been tied to an extremely thin string and, as she swallowed, the meat went down but the fine string remained tied to the hand of the healer who chanted and pulled on it while it was stuck down her throat, repeatedly ending with the question in a local dialect "Are you still in love with this boy?" to which the young lady always said "yes". After the third time, she finally realized that she was going to have to have this string lodged inside of her and pulled on until she admitted that the incantation and ritual had cured and cleansed her. Once she admitted that she was cured the string was cautiously but dangerously pulled out from within her with a swift and extremely painful yank and Dr. Soren drove her home. She was in considerable discomfort from a terribly sore throat which she clutched at repeatedly while groaning. Soren had thought of interfering with the ritual but it was so solemn and serious that he was afraid he would be arrested locally or worse if he interfered in any way. It should be added that this ended the love affair of the young couple permanently and everyone present believed that they had witnessed a healing doctor with supernatural power. This ceremony Dr. Soren experienced with his own eyes.

At Thurburbo Maius, near Fahs, hired Berber workmen excavators were terrified to dig deep trenches, fearful that they would enter into the underground lair of what they called the Djinn or a bloodthirsty bird-like vampire woman known as the Arbetha, who could carry off small children in the night and to whom table scrap offerings might be made after meals in the evening. Digging there would be accompanied by the wearing of protective amulets. And this was a project funded by the Smithsonian Institution and administered by the University of Iowa!

WITCHCRAFT IN HORACE: BROAD COMEDY AND STARK HORROR

And so it seems that we must allow ourselves the possibility that not everyone in every society ancient or modern sees its world through the same eyes. The poetry of Horace allows a window into the complex Augustan period attitudes about witchcraft. In the humorous Horace *Satire* I.8 we are treated to a bumbling and comical witch named Canidia and her companion Sagana frequenting the old graveyard which has been buried under by the newly developed Gardens of Maecenas on the eastern Esquiline Hill in Rome outside of the old city limits. In the moonlight, the two witches are looking for human bones and special herbs to use for their spells (*ossa herbasque nocentis*). The pale Canidia advances dressed in a black cloth, her feet bare and her hair let down, screaming along with the older and equally pale Sagana. In their search (I.8.25) they scratch at the earth with their fingernails or claws (*unguibus*).

The witches then (I.8.28) rip apart a black lamb with their teeth (*pullum divellere mordicus agnam coeperunt*) which is reminiscent of the puppies sacrificed in our cemetery with their mandibles literally ripped off from them. The purpose of Canidia and Sagana's endeavor is to pour the blood into furrows in the earth in order to receive answers from the chthonic spirits to their questions and to gain control of the liminal space between the living and the dead. Then the witches produce woolen and wax effigies, the former arranged somehow to seem to punish the latter in some mysterious rite. Of course such "dolls" were not able to be recovered from our cemetery if they existed due to the perishable materials from which they were made but a bone doll was in fact found, armless and legless. At this point in *Satire* I.8.35 the goddesses Hecate and Tisiphone are summoned, which brings forth snakes and hell hounds. In our cemetery there are 12 dogs, all puppies, and one immature dog, slaughtered and with several showing evidence of having the jaws ripped off. One puppy was cut in two and numerous puppy bones were found strewn about.

In the ceremony of evoking the spirits of the dead and conversing with them back and forth for nefarious purposes in the poem, there are some things mentioned that do not occur in our cemetery. Most of them may be due to the perishable nature of the items which could not be found: remains of snakes including the tooth of a mottled snake, the wax and woolen images and a shuddering doll. We cannot know any costumes or ritual dress that might have been worn, the treating of the face with ash or colorings and of course the use of animal blood, although our cemetery rituals were clearly bloody. In addition the possible mixing stone suggests that coloring or some sort of medicinal or apotropaic powder could have played a role in the services (Fig. 26).

The burning fires also cannot be localized in the cemetery but there are frequent ash pits throughout as well as two large bronze cauldrons which must have contained something boiling or burning in addition to the several varieties of wood found (Fig. 27). Not all of the finds from the cemetery match precisely to the description in *Satire* I.8 but the rites performed were not for the same reasons; nonetheless, the parallels are worth noting.

Certainly, witchcraft rites can vary from place to place and even from witch to witch (!) and in this case Horace is writing what amounts to virtually a slapstick comedy as Canidia loses her teeth when a statue of Priapus comes to life and farts, and Sagana drops her wig and the witches lose their herbs and enchanted arm bands! The events at Poggio Gramignano cemetery on the other hand are the result of a terrifying reality and yet the rites suggest that witchcraft, so comical in the one situation, was employed at our cemetery with serious fervor. And it is important to note that Horace's story is set in Rome in a public garden spot, not in some rural area where such credulity might be expected. Our infant cemetery was located within walking distance of a Tiber River harbor that would trade regularly downstream with Rome but it was situated on an abandoned hillside out of the way of big city or even rural town affairs.

FIGURE 26 Possible square slate mixing stone circa 8 cms per side, found near Burial 51.

FIGURE 27 Excavating the bronze cauldrons and surrounding ash layer.

Horace's *Satire* I.8 is not the only work of his to exhibit parallels with materials from our excavation. In his *Epode* V, written in 49 B.C., a darker side of Canidia and Sagana and other witches is revealed as they and several other witches seek to create a love potion to affect the charms of a certain Varus by capturing, torturing and starving to death a young boy. One witch, Veia, buries the boy alive up to his head in order to starve him to death within sight of food and to slowly dry out his liver and bone marrow in order to make the witches' love potion more effective.

Numerous accoutrements to the vile act are listed and Canidia's unkempt hair is referred to as bound with snakes. These accessories include uprooted fig trees, a feather and egg from an owl, the blood of a hideous frog along with poisonous herbs, and bones snatched from the mouth of a starving hound, all of which were mixed together and burned, supposedly in a large cauldron of some sort.[72] This extreme measure is done because Varus, the object of the witches' spells, is unresponsive to Canidia and it is reasoned that this is because other witches or demons had more powerful spells to keep this coven from achieving its ends.[73]

The young boy victim, sensing he will be killed by the witches, places a curse upon them and promises to become a revenant who will return from the dead to seek vengeance upon them as a "nocturnal fury/ *nocturnus furor*" who will "attack the witches in their sleep" and furthermore the "town people will stone the witches to death."[74] He adds that, as a living dead shade, he will "claw at their faces with hooked talons" because "such is the power of the gods of the dead"("petamque voltus umbra curvis unguibus quae vis deorum est manium") and the witches will be stoned by a mob on street after street and their unburied bodies will be torn apart by birds and wolves of the Esquiline Hill. And the boy's surviving parents will be witness to all of this horror and vengeance ("vos turba vicatim hic et hinc saxis petim contundit obscaenas anus post insepulta membra different lupi et Esquilinae alites, necque hoc parentes, heu mihi superstites, effugerit spectaculum").

Although this epode deals with the desire to make a love potion that can charm a male object of a witch's desire, it has some specific interest for the special rites occurring in our cemetery. Of course, again, many of the items cited in the epode were perishable and it cannot be determined if such things were used or not. However, among what we can determine, we see the strong involvement of dogs in the ritual along with frogs/toads (or at least their blood), probably some kind of cauldrons presumably to mix up the ingredients, an obsession with and danger to young dead or in this case a child seized, tortured and apparently about to be murdered by witches or demons, and the hooked talons of a bird which might be used by a revenant to claw at faces. All of the above may connect or relate to the rites discovered at Poggio Gramignano and of particular note is the statement made by the imperiled boy that he will himself become a revenant to wreak vengeance and horror when he comes back from the dead under the influence of the powerful gods of the dead. It is specifically this fear of the revenant, perhaps more than anything else, which seems to have gripped the Poggio Gramignano community and forced infant burials to be placed with stones in the mouth and stones and reused tiles over the body. Also much of the horror in *Epode V* is perceived to have occurred at night when there is the fear of the dark and the time when malarial fever is normally most intense.[75]

Epode V is all the more horrible because it ends without a positive resolution or for that matter without any resolution and we are left to think about a soon to exist child demon rising from the dead to seek vengeance among the living. In this case the child is seeking revenge against the witches who are torturing, starving and murdering him, but in the case of our Poggio Gramignano pandemic a demon or evil witch may have been thought to be terrorizing the community and to be capable of raising the dead to terrify all of the living. The fear at Poggio Gramignano was of the unknown and of the blurring of the line of the frightening liminality between the living and the dead exemplified by the cemetery.

ANCIENT LITERARY DEMONS

With regard to the terrorizing of infants and particularly those who have died in infancy, there is no shortage of demons cited in Roman literature. Much of this is of course tied to the difficulty of childbirth and the large numbers of infants who died. Since the Romans were a society which tended to personify its values, triumphs and fears, several popular candidates emerge for the child-killing and child-using demon, although we may never know the specific creature or creatures or know the local name for it/them in our ancient community. But we can start with a particularly odious feminine bird monster candidate known as the *strīx* (plural *striges*).[76]

A nocturnal *strix* (in this case referring to an owl) has already been mentioned in *Epode* V as providing Canidia with a feather and eggs smeared with the blood of a hideous frog.[77] *Strigae*, referring to demons and not owls, were already well known by the early second century B.C. when their first mention in Latin occurs in Plautus.[78] They are in fact female bird monsters who, according to Ovid have large heads, unblinking eyes and beaks made for hunting. Their wings are white and they have hooked talons.[79]

They fly at night looking for small children who have become separated from their nurses, pounce on the infants and tear out their entrails with their beaks and fill their gullets with imbibed blood. These insatiable harpies terrify with their strident bird shrieking in the night and are often identified with screech owls (also called *striges* in Latin) known to make piercing cries in defending their nests or when humans get too close to them. Their very name in Greek suggests a horrible scream. Ovid cites them as descendants of those terrifying harpies who menaced Phineus every time he tried to eat.[80]

The *strix* is also noted by the Roman grammarian Antoninus Liberalis, perhaps in the second century A.D., in his *Metamorphoseon Synagogue* or *Transformation Collection*, in this case perhaps derived from the *Ornithigonia* of Boios of probable fourth century B.C. date which dealt with the transformation of mythical figures into birds. Here the tale is told of virginal Polphonte whom Aphrodite made to fall in love with a bear which led to the birth of two giant cannibals. Zeus condemned all three, but Ares intervened and transformed them into birds with Polphonte becoming the *strix* that cries in the night without food or water and has its head located below its feet. One son became a *lagos* or bird of ill omen and the other a vulture with a constant desire for human flesh and blood.[81] A *strix* or something very much like it could be the alleged culprit for the child deaths in the Poggio Gramignano cemetery but it is far from being the only candidate.

Lilith is another female demon connected to birds of prey with a long and complicated history which may ultimately go back as far as the third millennium B.C. and who became widely known as a childless swift and silent nighttime abductor and murderer of children. Lilith was a particular threat to newborns and new mothers, especially around the home, because she would infest and infect the house, suck infant blood and ingest their bone marrow. Like many of these demons, she was also a shape-shifter, so much so that she could even take the place of the mother within the home and cause otherwise inexplicable deaths of children.[82] In order to defend against the creature all sorts of amulets and incantations were used. On the so-called Burney Relief from Sumer in the British Museum, datable to ca. 2000 B.C., a beautiful nude winged female is shown with feathered legs and fiercely sharp taloned feet. She stands on lions and is flanked by screech owls![83] (Figure 28; Figure 29).

The association of the unexplained, sudden and frightening attacks on a community attributed to demon bird-like// creatures are reminiscent of the Alfred Hitchcock 1963 movie *The Birds* where the group feeling of the terrorized community may carry an echo of what the community around Poggio Gramignano went through. The birds were viewed as harbingers of doom, attackers of children (and adults) and symbols of chaos, catastrophe and death, causing people to fear to go about freely, to question their understanding of their "normal" world, and to need to confine themselves within homes and even public buildings which themselves might not be safe. These ideas were brought home even more strongly in the original 1952 story by Daphne De Maurier, which was based on a real-life incident. And of course birds attack with talons, which are used to catch rats which contain disease-carrying micro-organisms that can infect wounds!

FIGURE 28 The Burney Relief from Sumer in the British Museum, datable to ca. 2000 B.C.

FIGURE 29 Graphic rendering of the Burney Relief

Yet another candidate for the demon of Poggio Gramignano is the *Lamia*, once in Greco-Roman mythology believed to be the Queen of Libya. She had an affair with Zeus and Hera took away her children, driving her mad and causing her to become envious of the children of others and to kidnap and devour infants at will. She became a monstrous creature often thought to be part snake. Her name may mean nocturnal spirit. For Aristotle, the *Lamia* was a monster shaped like a woman who tore open the bellies of pregnant women and devoured their fetuses, a sort of vampire-like creature sometimes equated with another demon named Mormo.[84] Since a *lamia* may generally be a child-killing demon, this of course may have parallels in the fear concerning the numerous stillbirths and miscarried fetuses caused by what we believe was *Plasmodium falciparum* malaria at our cemetery.

Another divinity who was mistress of the dark and of the graveyard and to whom liminal prayers might be offered for protection of babies was Hecate. She appears to be the number one candidate to receive prayers for the prevention of harm or help in a mystifying and terrifying crisis in part because she was known as a goddess who could lead the mortal dead through every threshold and ultimately back to the world of living and to normalcy, having served as the πρόπολος or path leader (with her torch to light the way through the darkness) and ὀπάων or companion and attendant for Persephone in the *Hymn to Demeter*, for example. She was also the protectress of crossroads often in triple bodied form and holding torches to see in all directions[85] (Figure 30). And it is she who was particularly associated with sacrificed dogs and the life and death of children in order to look out for the infant and the terror that could and often did ensue for the expectant mother. Although herself a lesser goddess, she was constantly working with other gods and goddesses as one who accompanies and assists and as such Hecate held influence over a number of birth goddesses perhaps due to her original role as a mother goddess in Greek literature, including the *Theogeny* of Hesiod.[86] Furthermore, she was a principal goddess of magic, witchcraft and protection from witchcraft, the night, the moon, ghosts and necromancy all of which make her fit in perfectly with the activities in the Poggio Gramignano cemetery. She is even specifically mentioned as we have seen in Horace's *Satire* I.8.35 as someone whom witches might frequently summon to help them, suggesting that she is a neutral goddess, a perpetual assistant who understands her role as an intermediary between living and dead, and between what is perceived as good and evil by mortals but not necessarily by the gods. In this role as interactor with the frightening world of demons and ghosts, she was prayed to by both families facing a crisis and witches/magicians because each group thought it would have a better chance of being successful in their request by persuading her to help them.[87]

She was the guardian of all entrances, especially to homes and especially at night, along with her portal-guarding dogs. As such she is often associated with keys and with the power to be the only one to lead people through unknown realms.[88] With her symbols of torches and her watchful constant companion dogs, she was, when appropriately honored, a protector of families, fulfilling much the same role as the Virgin Mary for many modern Christian communities when unforeseen and unexpected horrors occur.

These are just some of the appropriate demons and divinities that could have been invoked to explain the practices within the cemetery. The Romans had many names for particular female creatures or snatcher demons who were capable of wreaking havoc and that fact indicates a widespread fear of magic and witchcraft directed towards families and especially infants. *Veneficae* were simply women, not always supernatural, who used potions, drugs and especially poisons either for good or evil. The group included the fabled Medea who helped Jason in his quest for the golden fleece

FIGURE 30 Hekataion sculpture featuring the 3-sided Hecate with 4 hands holding torch and wearing polos crown (believed to be 3rd century A.D.) From the excavations at Perge (Turkey). Now in the Antalya Archaeological Museum, Turkey.

but whose jealous rage over her husband's marital indiscretion led her to poison her own children whom she had had with the hero.[89]

Meroe in Apuleius' *Metamorphoses*, written in the later second century, was a lustful innkeeper and monster, like a vampire. She slit throats, drained blood, clawed out hearts, urinated on the friend of a deceased person, and restored the dead to life unless they were able to drink water in which case they would become a ghastly bloodless corpse. The work by Apuleius is full of creatures with magical powers and Meroe at her worst supposedly even had the ability to pull down the heavens, turn rivers to stone and mountains to water, be a shapeshifter, lay low the gods, snuff out stars, and brighten Tartarus, the dungeon of the souls of the condemned dead.[90]

The *Metamorphoses* may be read as almost a parody of more ancient epic tales such as those spun by Homer and it may also be seen as an avant-garde or what has been called a neoteric approach to fantasy story-telling.[91] But what is of more concern for our interests is the use of demons, shape-shifters (note the title of the work), witches and constant uncertainties about this period of Roman life especially in the provinces outside of Rome. Furthermore, Apuleius' world was also colored by the fact that he himself had been formally accused of practicing black magic and using love charms and even magic fish to seduce a wealthy widow to marry him, as is cited in his *Apologia*.[92]

In the *Metamorphoses*, not only do the living have to fear being used by witches for illicit purposes, but pregnant women must fear the wrath of Meroe who could prevent pregnancies if someone only spoke harsh words against her. Meroe was able to close up wombs and, in one of Apuleius' wildest flights of fantasy, render a woman everlastingly pregnant with the result that after eight years she would swell up so much as to be capable of delivering a great elephant.[93] But this bizarre and unsavory passage can also be read as a reflection of the fear of the unknown and of witchcraft among some citizens and not necessarily only those in rural areas.

Circe in Homer's *Odyssey* 10 was yet another dreadful goddess with lovely hair who was able to cause the shapeshifting of humans into animals and who through potions and herbs could reanimate the dead. She was even considered a daughter of Hecate by Diodorus Siculus in an odd variation of her traditional origins, and she allowed Odysseus to speak with deceased humans in the underworld after he would perform the proper rituals and pour blood into a cup to attract their shades, although she was more of a literary figure than a possible agent of immediate fear for the citizens of Poggio Gramignano.[94]

Still another dangerous figure, perhaps the most terrifying of all, was Erictho, the hideous Thessalian witch (*Thessala vates*) of Lucan's epic about the Roman Civil War, *Pharsalia*[95] 6.413-774, who was also said to be able to reanimate the dead. In 48 B.C., Sextus Pompey was fighting with Pompey the Great and troops ordered by the Roman senate against Julius Caesar when Sextus allegedly sought to know the outcome of the battle of Pharsalus in central Greece by making a direct request to this most prominent of Thessalian witches and visiting her home at night. In all of Latin literature the description of her and her activities may be the most disgusting and depraved and in the *Pharsalia*, Lucan describes her supposed practices in lurid detail. She found and filled a dead body with poisons and reanimated it in order to have it give a prophecy about the Pharsalus battle along with an account of strife occurring within the underworld.[96] She was one of a long line of fearful Thessalian witches who were believed to have the power to reanimate the underworld itself. Although she too may have been intended as a literary invention, perhaps by Ovid originally and continued by Lucan in the 60s C.E., the actual widespread fear in the general populace of necromancers and demon witches wreaking havoc in the world and creating revenants shines through.

Erictho is described as hellish, vile and haggard in appearance with unkempt hair and poisonous breath. She delights in burying still living bodies which have not attained their allotted span of years and she also reanimates corpses. Thus, she is of particular danger to children, even snatching their bones from a funeral pyre before it can be fully consecrated, and taking the torches for lighting the fire from the hands of the child's parents. She desecrates all manner of bodies, gouging out their eyes and gnawing off their yellowed fingernails. For crucified victims she even takes out the nails that were piercing through their hands and sucks out any accumulated gore from the corpse.

For children, however, her ravages are particularly horrid, including piercing the womb of a pregnant woman and extracting the child in order to burn it at an altar.[97] This may have been one reason that the pregnant women of Poggio Gramignano would have had fear for their stillborn and prematurely delivered babies. And as to a possible reason for putting a stone in the mouth of the deceased there is this Lucan passage[98]:

> Saepe etiam caris cognato in funere dira Thessalis incubuit membris atque oscula figens truncauitque caput conpressaque dentibus ora laxauit siccoque haerentem gutture linguam praemordens gelidis infudit murmura labris arcanumque nefas Stygias mandauit ad umbras.

> "Often too, when a loved one is buried, the dreadful witch will hang over the body in kissing it, mutilates the head, opens the closed mouth with her teeth, bites the tip of the inert tongue in the dry mouth, infuses the cold lips with murmuring sound, and sends a wicked and arcane message down to the Stygian shades."

Thus it may be that a stone in the mouth might both protect a buried individual from having the mouth being invaded by a witch for nefarious purposes and it might also protect the living from being attacked by a revenant bringing evil and danger.

A Greek demon of special interest here is the dreaded Gello, herself a revenant, who threatened women's reproductive capabilities by causing infertility, miscarriage and infant death.[99] A woman deemed to be under the influence of this demon might be considered impure, brought to trial or forced to undergo a purification ritual. At least as far back as the sixth century B.C. this creature was a source of horror to children and is the sort of figure that might be used to force small children to listen more carefully to their parents!

Mormo was another divinity invoked to frighten children, originally believed to be a Corinthian woman who devoured her own children and who was later considered part of a group of hideous spectres who menaced children particularly.[100] One may also mention the *empusa* who, despite having an abnormal leg, primarily sought to attack young men and who could change shape dramatically (from ox to mule to beautiful young woman to bitch). Her interest in young flesh and her identification as a spectre or ghost and her relationship to Hecate especially allow her to be included here as another possibility, at least in relatively late sources. The *empousae* are *phasmata* or phantoms that Hecate can send forth as a ghostly inhibitor.[101] It should be noted that these demon names were able to be used somewhat interchangeably to suggest an evil female demon, although different demons might be averted by various ritual practices.[102] But one could be called an *empusa* or a *strix* or a *mormo* with little distinction just because one had done an evil act.

For protection from the fear of the death of babies and mothers there were also a host of apotropaic birthing divinities/personifications who could be prayed to and who looked after every different detail no matter how minute, of the birth, development and healthful growth of a child. These divinities are too many to list here but one can briefly mention *Mana Genita* who was particular important for the mortality of the baby and its actual successful birth and it is of particular interest here that her rites included puppy or bitch sacrifice and a direct connection with Hecate if she is not to be considered an aspect of Hecate herself. A prayer might also be offered to her that no other members of the household become dead.[103] There was also the *Candelifera* or candle-bearing goddess who might help keep the evil spirits of the night and darkness from harming the birthing mother and the child and who might help to bring the child safely into the light of the world.[104]

Along with the threat of demons and witches was the threat of ghosts or what Sarah Iles Johnston has referred to as "restless dead", such as the *mors immatura* or those dead before their appropriate life span. Such individuals could become ghosts known in Greece as the *aoroi* and were most often spirits of children and infants, the word deriving from αωροσ meaning untimely.[105] The spirits may be termed restless due to the miserable gloom in which many are perceived to dwell and the failure of the individuals to reach their life potential; as such they would wish to return to the world of the living. Furthermore, they or more precisely their unspent life force would be fair game for witches to harness as a powerful catalyst for potions or whatever evil they might wish to perpetrate. And of course newly dead children or children as yet unborn would therefore be targets of choice. It is for these reasons that the newly born or the as yet unborn had to be protected particularly in times of trouble in a community so that techniques ranging from necromancy to physically weighing down childrens' corpses with stones, and the use of prayers and elaborate rituals needed to be employed by a religious leader particularly skilled in apotropaic necromancy and the protection of the dead.

Although the persecution of so-called pagan religion in the Roman Empire began in a more systematic manner in the fourth century AD[106], culminating with its being outlawed by Theodosius' decree in 392, literary and archaeological sources indicate that paganism, its related rituals, and a belief in witchcraft survived. The deep belief in the existence of witches and magic is clear through various literary sources as well as in the archaeological evidence. The reliance of ancient magic on ghosts and goddesses such as Hecate makes this topic particularly relevant to the study of a cemetery such as that at Poggio Gramignano. Witches, necromancy, and restless spirits could all have been viewed logically at the time as tangible threats to the community using the cemetery at Lugnano. The pregnant mothers and midwives involved in dealing with the deaths of the infants in the cemetery could have believed in and feared supernatural interference in the pregnancies, miscarriages and early deaths. They also faced a post-mortem fear of disturbance of the burials due to ingredients used in magic rituals by dangerous spirits. These rituals might have been thought to include an invocation of *aoroi* spirits to do the bidding of witches, or even attacks from the restless spirits themselves as revenants.

CONCLUSION

So what were the local villagers afraid of in the cemetery at Poggio Gramignano about 450 A.D. or slightly thereafter? The *Plasmodium falciparum* pandemic which we believe occurred at this time was apparently something new and terrifying, perhaps the result of a perfect storm of exceptionally warm summer conditions, transport vessels bringing wine in amphorae coming from North Africa where malaria was well known, and a Tiber waterway that had become more difficult to patrol and control and which likely contained some areas of standing water that were a fine breeding ground for mosquitoes. Despite the fact that the area was at least nominally Christian by this time with a bishopric in nearby Amelia, it must have been felt that that this religion was not providing immediate answers for the distraught community and a revitalization movement was imposed which saw the revival of traditional belief systems, triggered by the pressing need to save lives and resolve the mystery of increasing deaths. The cemetery excavations revealed single burials at the lowest levels escalating into multiple burials as the level of earth grew higher over the summer days, with all of the interments in soft ashy earth and with joins from top to bottom in the pottery.

A divinity such as Hecate or a more local equivalent offered hope and eventual seeming success since she was a goddess familiar with the horrible and the chthonic and if approached correctly could be not only a companion for both the living and the dead but also a savior or *soteira* for the entire community.[107] This approach appeared to work because a malaria epidemic, limited to the particular conditions of a warm later July to August of circa 450 A.D. could not have endured into fall, and the epidemic eased gradually. When the epidemic was at its height, fear of revenants, the reanimated dead, was such that deceased infants needed to be weighed down and stones put in their mouths to avert the spread of evil in the community. This seems to have been done for two of the older children found, suggesting that a child old enough to be buried with his or her mouth able to be opened significantly got a stone and the older the infant the greater the fear for its peaceful rest in the grave and its possible reappearance as a revenant.

A whole history of terrifying demons could have elicited this great fear in the community as the motivators of the actions taken at the cemetery. The citizens used stones in the mouth, weighing down the bodies with tile and stone, a toad, a raven's talon, possibly iron nails and a dismembered doll, 13 dog sacrifices of which 12 were puppies 5 to 6 months old and themselves virtually *aoroi*, not allowed to finish their own lives and in fact having their jaws ripped off and in one case with a body severed in two. In addition portions of puppies appear to have been scattered about perhaps due to a lack of sufficient whole puppies to sacrifice in the community and associate with the burials. The puppy offerings may also have been intended as offerings, as cited earlier, to birthing goddesses associated with Hecate such as *Eilithyia* and *Genetyllis* and *Candelifera* in order to appease them and prevent them from destroying future issue as well as protecting the souls of the already dead. Perhaps the unusual finding of the broken bronze candelabrum, possible palette, *dolabra* and cow skull were part of a ceremony related to one of these deities.

Not coincidentally the period of mid summer was traditionally a time of significant stress in communities in general. The period between July 10 and August 15 is known even now as the Dog Days of Summer and in antiquity were the days of the influence of the dog star Sirius and termed the *caniculae* or days of the little dog. Even as far back as the time of Hesiod, it was said that Sirius dries up the head and knees and the skin gets parched by the burning heat. *Seiriasis* was an actual ancient disease believed to be caused by the Dog Star Sirius and resulted in inflammation of the meninges accompanied by a burning fever.[108]

The finding of the upper portion of a bronze lamp stand buried along with a cow skull and axe-head of an iron *dolabra* suggests a night ritual involving the sacrifice and beheading of a cow, and the discovery with these objects of what could be a slate mixing slab for pigments or some sort of medicinal concoction adds to the mystery of the precise service occurring here. The large amount of piglet bones found suggest ritual meals and may also indicate offerings to birthing goddesses and/or to appease demons. The presence of two cooking pots placed upside down containing mammal scrap could reflect offerings to chthonic deities while the two large copper alloy cauldrons imply that something special was being burned or mixed up in addition to the various types of woods recovered. In several areas significant amounts of *Lonicera caprifolium* or honeysuckle were found and this as we have seen was touted by Pliny as an aid for splenomegaly which was a symptom of *Plasmodium falciparum* malaria. Numerous other deposits of burned woods and plants were recovered, among them the foul-smelling buckthorn believed to be a deterrent to demons.

We cannot know the name of the precise demon believed to be responsible for the terror but there were certainly plenty of possible creatures to choose from, including various types of *strix*. A number of these demon monsters have in common that they are bird-like child stealers and menaces to pregnant women and they have enormous power to disrupt and terrify a community. Furthermore, they can shape-shift so it is difficult to know whom you can really trust in your community…or who might be under their influence.

From these discoveries at Poggio Gramignano, it is also possible to take a fresh look at Horace in particular and realize that the witchcraft practices he talked about in his poetry were not just literary conceits or comic inventions as has often been suggested but must have seemed very real to many people from early Roman times to the later Roman Empire and beyond. The hideous demons presented in Horace, Lucan, Apuleius and other ancient sources may have been intended to amuse, entertain and influence popular and scholarly readers with fantastic stories but it appears clear from the physical evidence obtained from our infant cemetery that much of what was written about in these fantastic stories appeared real to a community that suddenly found itself face to face with the terrifying unknown.

Endnotes

1- "What It Feels Like to Have Malaria," *Gates Blog* by Bill Gates. April 25, 2014. https://www.gatesnotes.com/What-Malaria-Feels-Like-Mosquito-Week

2- Lara Zekar, Tariq Sharman, "Plasmodium falciparum Malaria" *National Institutes of Health National Library of Medicine* 8-8-2022 https://www.ncbi.nlm.nih.gov/books/NBK555962/; Joan Stivala, "Malaria and miscarriage in ancient Rome," *Canadian Bulletin of Medical History* 32(1) 2015 pp. 143-161 in which the author claims that aborted fetuses were not so commonly induced as they were the result of miscarriages caused by diseases such as especially malaria. Current research by Hendrik Poynar and Stephanie Marciniak will hopefully elucidate more definitively soon the question of the presence of *Plasmodium falciparum* at Poggio Gramignano's cemetery. It is possible that *Plasmodium vivax* and even other diseases such as cholera may have also been present.

3- David Soren, "Can Archaeologists Excavate Evidence of Malaria," *World Archaeology*, Vol. 35 No. 2 2003 pp. 193-209; David Soren, Todd Fenton, Walter Birkby, "The Late Roman Infant Cemetery near Lugnano in Teverina, Italy: some implications," *Journal of Palaeopathology* 7 (1) 1995 pp. 13-42; Robert Sallares, *Malaria and Rome: A History of Malaria in Ancient Italy* (Oxford University Press, 2002); Sallares and S. Gomzl, "Biomolecular Archaeology of Malaria," *Ancient Biomolecules* 3 (3) 2001 pp. 195-213; Sallares, Abigail Bouwman, Cecilia Anderung, "The Spread of Malaria to Southern Europe in Antiquity: New Approaches to Old Problems," *Medical History* 48 2004 pp. 311-328 and especially pp. 319-322 on the direct evidence from the Lugnano in Teverina excavations; Jamie Inwood, "Identifying Malaria in Ancient Human Remains: An Investigation Into the Interactions Between Ancient Disease and Population Dynamics," Ph.D. Dissertation, Yale University 2017; Jamie Inwood, "Malaria Test Developed for Ancient Human Remains," *Archaeology* (AIA News) 3-17-2015. https://www.archaeology.org/news/3089-150317-malaria-parasite-bone/ ; Jim Shelton, "Creating a malaria test for ancient human remains," *Yale News* 3-17-2015

4- Jordan P. Wilson, "Negotiating Infant Parenthood in Death: Interpreting Atypical Burials in the Late Roman Infant and Child Cemetery at Poggio Gramignano (Italy)," *American Journal of Archaeology* 125.2 2022 p. 223.

5- For current data on malaria see UNICEF data child health on the internet. The date of ca. 450 is determined from the pottery and oil lamps recovered from the site, and also from the account of traveler Sidonius Apollinaris in A.D. 467 reporting what still appeared to be a malarial zone encountered along the Via Flaminia (*Epp.* 1.5 to 1.7). We have also argued that that Pope Leo I was able to discourage Attila the Hun from invading Rome in 452 because he pointed out the danger of widespread disease to Attila and his troops if he proceeded and it is recorded that his troops were already ill at this time. On this see Frank Romer, "Famine, Pestilence and Brigandage in Italy in the Fifth Century A.D.," in David and Noelle Soren, *A

Roman Villa and a Late Roman Infant Cemetery (L'Erma di Bretschneider, 1999) p. 472; see also Andrew Thompson, "Malaria and the Fall of Rome," *BBC Website* 2-17-2011. https://www. bbc.co.uk/history/ancient/romans/malaria_01.shtml

6-   For the tomb types see David Soren, Todd Fenton, Walter Birkby, "The Infant Cemetery at Poggio Gramignano: Description and Analysis," in Soren and Soren pp. 490-491 and more recently Wilson 2022 p. 236; Jazz Demetrioff, "Malaria's Breeding Grounds and Effects on Ancient Rome," *Past Imperfect* Vol. 22 No. 1 2020 pp. 1-30. For the types of amphorae see Archer Martin, "Amphorae" in Soren and Soren pp. 329-362.

7-   For Roman *suggrundaria* burials and burials of infants within hillforts, villas, workshops and dwelling places, see Maureen Carroll, *Infancy and Earliest Childhood in the Roman World: 'A Fragment of Time'* (Oxford University Press 2018) p. 163. Apparently both burials in *suggrundaria* fashion and in separated adult and infant/child cemeteries happened to varying degrees on various sites. In addition to Carroll's pointing this out, see C. Tassinari, "Archeologia funeraria a Colombarone (PU): il suggrundarium tardoantico. Caratteri e problematiche di un rituale funerario", *Ocnus* XIV 2006 pp. 303-308.

8-   On these practices see Soren, Fenton and Birkby 1998 p. 526.; Maureen Carroll, "Infant Death and Burial in Roman Italy." *Journal of Roman Archaeology* 24, no. 2 (2011) pp. 99-120 and especially pages 102-104. Carroll suggests a mortality rate of as much as 50% before the age of 10; see also J. Pearce,. "Infants, Cemeteries and Communities in the Roman Provinces." In *TRAC 2000: Proceedings of the Tenth Annual Theoretical Roman Archaeology Conference*, edited by D. Davies, A. Gardner, and K. Lockyear. (Oxford: Oxbow, 2001) pp.125–42; A. B. Scott and T.K. Betsinger. "Excavating Identity: Burial Context and Fetal Identity in Post-Medieval Poland." In *The Anthropology of the Fetus: Biology, Culture, and Society*, edited by S. Han, A.B. Scott, and T.K. Betsinger (New York: Berghahn 2017) pp. 146-168. Gowland et al suggest 30% infant mortality rate in Rebecca L. Gowland, A. Chamberlain, and Rebecca C. Redfern.. "On the Brink of Being: Re-evaluating Infanticide." *Journal of Roman Archaeology Suppl. 96* 2014 pp. 69–88.

9-   The Council of Carthage in A.D. 252 decreed that infants were to be included in Christian burials and not discarded since the newly born, "free from actual sin", had to be baptized and thus were formally entered into the faith. Cyprian, *Epist.* 55. On care of Christian newborns see É. Rebillard, *The Care of the Dead in Late Antiquity*. Ithaca: Cornell University Press 2010) p. 174.

10- Eleanor Scott, "Animal and Infant Burials in Romano-British Villas: A Revitalization Movement," in P. Garwood, D. Jennings, R. Skeates and J. Toms, *Sacred and Profane: Proceedings of a Conference on Archaeology, Ritual and Religion at Oxford* (Oxford University Committee for Archaeology 1991 pp. 116-121. R. Linton, "Nativistic Movements," *American Anthropologist* 45 no. 1 1943 pp. 230-240. For a discussion of medical anthropology theory and the need to avoid assessing ancient situations as if they were being approached by modern people, see C. Rosenburg,. "Disease in history: frames and framers." *The Milbank Quarterly*, Vol. 67, No. 1 1989 pp. 1-15; J. Arrizabalaga, "Problematizing retrospective diagnosis in the history of disease." *Asclepio: Archivo Iberoamericano de Historia de La Medicina y Antropologia Medica*, Vol. 54, No. 1 2002 pp. 51–70. https://doi.org/10.3989/asclepio.2002.v54.i1.135

11- Plutarch, *Consolatio ad uxorem*. For the new viewpoint see Maureen Carroll, "Infant Death and Burial in Roman Italy." *Journal of Roman Archaeology* 24, no. 2 2011 p. 100. See also Han Baltussen, "Personal Grief and Public Mourning in Plutarch's 'Consolation to His Wife'," *The American Journal of Philology* Vol. 130, No. 1 Spring, 2009, pp. 67-98.

12- Maureen Carroll 2018 pp. 147-177 on the *mors immatura*; Naomi J. Norman, "Death and burial of Roman children: the case of the Yasmina cemetery at Carthage—part I, setting the stage," *Mortality* 7, no. 3 (2002) pp. 302-323; Wilson 2022 pp. 219-241.

13- Wilson 2022 p. 220

14- Wilson 2022 p. 222; Plutarch, *Numa* 12; Paulus, *Pauli Sententiae* 1.21.13-14; Cicero, *Tusculanae Disputationes* 1.93; Ulpian, *Fontes Iuris Romani Anteiustiniani* 2.536;

15- Juvenal, *Satires* 15.139; Pliny the Elder, *Naturalis Historia* 7.68-7.72.

16- Plutarch, *Consolatio ad uxorem* 6; Seneca, *Ad Lucilium Epistulae Morales* 99; Tacitus *Annales* 15.23; Carroll 2011 p. 100.

17- Plutarch *Consolatio ad uxorem* 3.

18- Statius *Thebaid* 4. 76-95; Virgil *Aeneid* 6.426-29.

19- Émile Jobbé-Duval, *Les morts malfaisants*, (Paris: Recueil Sirey, 1924)

20- Carroll 2011 p. 106

21- Carroll 2011 p. 108

22- This procedure was set up in consultation with then University of Arizona colleague Michael Brian Schiffer, following his *Formation Processes of the Archaeological Record* (University of New Mexico Press, 1987)

23- David Soren, Todd Fenton and Walter Birkby, "The Infant Cemetery at Poggio Gramignano: Description and Analysis," in Soren and Soren 1999 p. 501. Also, see Wilson 2022 p. 236 who writes "Oddly similar, Soren and Soren (1999, 481) describe an unpublished excavation by Marshall Joseph Becker at Avallone in Pontecagnano near Salerno, Italy, 1991, wherein three amphora burials of infants were found in association with an unspecified foot phalanx (toe bone) from an adolescent 14 to 17 years old." On the generally positive Roman attitude to the birth of twins, see Veronique Dasen, "Blessing or Portents: Multiple Births in Ancient Rome," in K. Mustakellio, J. Hanska, H.-L. Sainio, V. Vuolonto (editors*), Hoping for Continuity. Childhood, Education and Death in Antiquity and the Middle Ages* (Acta Instituti Romani Finlandiae XXIII, Rome 2005) 72-83. But we do not know the attitude toward twin births when they are both born dead.

24- Special thanks to Sarah Iles Johnston for this information. See also Sarah Iles Johnston, *Restless Dead* (Berkeley: University of California Press 1999) chapter 3 on the function of the *goes* and his ability to communicate with and pacify the restless dead. She also distinguished a *goes* from a *magus* who is less commonly connected with invocation of the spirit of the dead.

25- Archer Martin, "Additional Small Finds" in Soren and Soren p. 445

26- For ravens and puppies at Dorchester, Winchester, and especially Oakridge where the burials were in association with 7 adult dogs and 87 puppies) see Dale Serjeanston and James Morris, "Ravens and Crows in Iron Age and Roman Britain," *Oxford Journal of Archaeology* 30 (1) 2011 pp. 85-107) and especially page 95.

27- M. J. Green, *Animals in Celtic Life and Myth* London 1992 177-181 and Serjeantson pp. 96, 99-100; Derek Radcliffe, *The Raven* (London: T and A.D. Poyser, 1997 p. 10); Soren and Soren plate 234; Soren, Fenton and Birkby p. 495. Pliny the Elder, *Natural history*, X.60.121-124 recounts the popularity of ravens in Rome as talking birds and fine pets that were particularly beloved by their owners and had distinguished funerals.

28- Soren and Soren plate 235

29- Michael McKinnon, "Animal Bone Remains," Soren and Soren p. 550; Garth H. Gilmour, "The Nature and Function of Astragalus Bones from Archaeological Contexts in the Levant and Eastern Mediterranean," *Oxford Journal of Archaeology* 17 December 2002 pp. 167-175. Jacopo De Grossi Mazzorin and Claudia Minniti, "Ancient Use of the knuckle-bone for rituals and gaming piece," *Anthropozoologica* 48 (2) 2013 pp. 371-390 and especially p. 377.

30- Leslie Shumka, "A Bone Doll from the Infant Cemetery at Poggio Gramignano," in Soren and Soren pp. 615-618. See also Soren, Fenton and Birkby in Soren and Soren 1999 p. 500.

31- Pliny *NH.* 27.94.120; Soren, Fenton and Birkby in Soren and Soren 1999 p. 523

32- Soren, Fenton and Birkby in Soren and Soren 1999 p. 496.

33- Martin, Small Finds in Soren and Soren 1999 p. 449

34- On votive nails, see Silvia Alfaye Villa, "Nails for the Dead: A Polysemic Account of an Ancient Funerary Practice," in Richard L. Gordon, Francisco Marco Simon, editors, *Magical Practice in the Latin West: Papers from the International Conference Held at the University of Zaragasa, 30 Sept.-1ˢᵗ October 2005* (Brill: Leiden, 2010) pp. 427-456. See also M. G. Maioli, "Magia e superstizione" in J. Ortalli and D. Neri (editors), *Immagini divine. Devozioni e divinità nella vita quotidiana dei Romani, testimonianze archeo-logiche dall'Emilia Romagna* (Bologna, 2007) p. 108. In Lucan the necromancer Erictho removes iron nails pinning down the hands of the dead, thus rendering this attempt to defend the living from the dead unsuccessful (Lucan, *Pharsalia* 6. 413-587. On this see Maureen Carroll, "Infant Death and Burial in Roman Italy." *Journal of Roman Archaeology* 24, no. 2 (2011) p.108. On the protective power of iron, see Pliny the Elder *Hist. Nat.* XXXIV.XLIV who notes that a fence of iron nails extracted from tombs and driven in front of the threshold of a home can protect one from having nightmares.

35- Giuseppina Borghetti "Consistenza dei reperti di vetro della villa di Poggio Gramignano," in Soren and Soren p. 403 no. 59 Plate 229.

36- On upside-down pots placed as a ritual feasting characteristic see Crawford Greenewalt and Sebastian Payne, *Ritual Dinners in Early Historic Sardis* (Berkeley: University of California Press, 1978) p. 55.

37- See Johnston 1999 p. 64 for the chewing of buckthorn to avert ghosts during the day of the dead festival known as the *Anthesteria* in Athens. Even today buckthorn has connections to magic and witchcraft posted throughout the internet, perhaps due to its foul smell.

38- MacKinnon in Soren and Soren 1999 p. 540. For the use of a female piglet to save Proca from being snatched, see Ovid *Fasti* 6.143-144; 159-162 and Maxwell Teitel Paule, *Canidia, Rome's First Witch* (Bloomsbury: London, 2018) pp. 67-70 on the Proca story in Ovid. See also below here footnote 76 and Varro *RR* II.4.15; Pliny *Hist. Nat.* VII.77.206. For ritual uses of dog sacrifice and dogs as guardians see also V. Amoretti, C. Bassi C. and A. Fontana, "Associated stillborn and dog burials: the uncommon case of the cemetery of Via Tommaso Gar (TN)" in Valentino Nizzo (ed.), *Archeologia e Antropologia a confront: archeologia e antropologia della morte 1: La regola dell'eccezione. Atti del Terzo Incontro Internazionale di studi* (AntArc: Rome) pp. 319-330

39- MacKinnon p. 545

40- MacKinnon pp. 542-543

41- MacKinnon pp. 548-549. A recent independent article on the dog (and particularly puppy) finds of the Poggio Gramignano / Lugnano in Teverina site can be found in Giulia Pedrucci, "Cuccioli di uomo, cuccioli di cane. Nuove proposte per l'interpretazione del materiale proveniente dalla necropoli di Lugnano in Teverina", in C. Terranova (editor), *La presenza dei bambini nelle religioni del Mediterraneo antico. La vita e la morte, i rituali e i culti tra archeologia, antropologia e storia delle religioni* (Aracne: Rome, 2014) pp. 185-216

42- "Symbolism and Mortuary Practice. Dogs in Fractions- Symbols in Action," *Archaeology and Environment* 11 1991 pp. 33-38. See also Greenewalt and Payne 1978.

43- MacKinnon p. 549; see also Virgil, *Aeneid* XII.753.

44- Barbara Wilkens, "The Sacrifice of Dogs in Ancient Italy," in Lynn M. Snyder, Elizabeth A. Moore (editors), *Dogs and People in Social, Working, Economic or Symbolic Interaction* (Oxbow Books, Oxford 2006) pp. 131-136; (no author), "Dog burial as common ritual in Neolithic populations of north-eastern Iberian Peninsula," *Science Daily* 2-14-2019 https://www.sciencedaily.com/releases/2019/02/190214153031.htm

45- Gillian Clark, "Philosophers' Pets: Porphyry's Partridge and Augustine's Dog," in T. Fögen and E. Thomas, *Interactions between Animals and Humans in Graeco-Roman Antiquity* (Walter de Gruyter: Berlin, 2017) p. 139

46- Columella, *De Re Rustica*, 7.1-14

47- Pliny, *Nat. Hist.*, Volume I: Books 1-2, Translated by H. Rackham. Loeb Classical Library 330, Cambridge, MA: Harvard University Press, 1938. On Alexander the Great's dog see Pliny, *Nat. Hist.* 8.147.

48- Xenophon, *Cynegeticus* (Hunting with Dogs); Arrian 5.1-2. Sian Lewis, "A Lifetime Together? Temporal Perspectives on Animal–Human Interactions," in Thorsten Fögen and Edmund Thomas (editors), *Interactions between Animals and Humans in Graeco-Roman Antiquity* (Berlin: De Gruyer, 2007) p. 19.

49- Clark, Gillian, T. Fögen, and E. Thomas. "Philosophers' pets: Porphyry's partridge and Augustine's dog." in Fögen and Thomas 2007 p. 101.

50- Michael MacKinnon and Kyle Belanger, "In sickness and in health: care for an arthritic Maltese dog from the Roman cemetery of Yasmina, Carthage, Tunisia," in Snyder, Moore et al 2006 p. 40.

51- Wilkens 2006 pp. 132-133

52- Maria A. Liston, Susan I. Rotroff, and Lynn M. Snyder, *The Agora Bone Well* (*Hesperia* Suppl. 50). (American School of Classical Studies at Athens, Princeton 2018). On dog sacrifice generally see Nicola Zaganiaris, "Sacrifices de chien dan l'antiquité Classique," *Platon* 27 1975 pp. 322-329, and also Jacopo De Grossi Mazzarin and Claudia Minniti, "Dog Sacrifice in the Ancient World: A Ritual Passage," in L.M. Snyder and E.A. Moore (eds.), *Dogs and People in Social, Working, Economic or Symbolic Interaction, 9th ICAZ Conference, Durham 2002* (University of Durham, 2006) pp. 62-66. On dog sacrifice near to Lugnano in Teverina in the late antique period, see Francesca Alhaique and Michele Tommaso Fortunato, "Possible evidences for a Dog Sacrifice at Ferento (Viterbo) in the Late Antique Period," Annali dell'Università degli Studi di Ferrara, Sezione di Museologia Scientifica e Naturalistica volume 11 n. 2 (2015) pp. 109-114. For the connection of dog sacrifice, Hecate and birth goddesses with complete documentation of ancient sources, see Johnston 1999 pp. 211-212.

53- Bettina Bergman, "The Roman House as Memory Theater: The House of the Tragic Poet in Pompeii," *The Art Bulletin* Vol. 76, No. 2 (June, 1994) pp. 225-256. For dog burials with infants see also David Miles (ed.), *Archaeology at Barton Court Farm, Abingdon, Oxon, Oxford Archaeology Unit* (Oxford 1986) pp. 15, 84-85. For an overview of 3 late antique cemeteries and the function of their dog and infant burials (Lugnano in Teverina, Peltuinum and Colombarone), see Lidia Vitale, "Sleeping with the dogs: animal sacrifices in the infant cemeteries. Examples from Late-Antiquity Italian necropoleis," Presentation Summary for *The Society for the Study of Childhood in the Past. 10th International Conference: The life and Death of children in the past. November, 6th – 10th 2017, Templo Mayor Museum, Mexico City*. Courtesy of the Department of Ancient World Studies, University of Rome, La Sapienza.

54- Alessio Sassù, "Through impurity: a few remarks on the role of the dog in purification rituals of the Greek world", in P. A. Johnston - A. Mastrocinque - S. Papaioannou (eds.), *Animals in Greek and Roman Religion and Myth*, (Newcastle upon Tyne: Cambridge Scholars Publishing, 2016), pp. 393-418 and especially 396-399.

55- Plutarch *Quaest. Rom.* 280c and J. De Grossi Mazzorin, "L'uso dei cani nei riti funerari. Il caso della necropoli di età imperiale a Fidene - via Radicofani", in M. Einzelmann et al. (eds.), *Rö-*

mischer Bestattungsbrauch und Beigabensitten in Rom, Norditalien und den Nordwestprovinzen von der späten Republik bis in die Kaiserzeit. Internationales Kolloquium Rom, 1-3 April 1998 (Reichert, Wiesbaden 2001) pp. 77-82. Varro *RR* II.4.15; Pliny *Hist. Nat.* VII.77.206. For ritual uses of dog sacrifice and dogs as guardians see also Amoretti V., Bassi C., Fontana A., "Associated stillborn and dog burials: the uncommon case of the cemetery of Via Tommaso Gar (TN)" in Valentino Nizzo (ed.), *Archeologia e Antropologia a confront: archeologia e antropologia della morte 1: La regola dell'eccezione. Atti del Terzo Incontro Internazionale di studi* (Ant-Arc: Rome) pp.319-330.

56- On atypical burial procedures in general see A. Taylor, A. "Aspects of Deviant Burial in Roman Britain." in E.M. Murphy (editor), *Deviant Burial in the Archaeological Record.* (Oxford: Oxbow 2008) pp. 91–114 and especially p.100. Burial 36 was initially identified as female but this has been called into question by our new research and awaits further confirmation.

57– The small slate stone had a small central depression which was interpreted as just large enough and deep enough to possibly mix something light but further comparative research is necessary. On a Roman ritual offering of a cow skull together with puppies at the site of Hatch Furlong in Ewell, England, 12 miles south of London, see https://www.yourlocalguardian. co.uk/news/11351869.suspected-roman-ritual-pit-found-in-archaeological-dig-in-ewell/ , *Guardian* 7-18-2014. On the cow / ox skull as a traditional Greco-Roman sacrificial image, see Calder Loth, "Bucrania," *Institute of Classical Architecture and Art* (Online) June 13, 2013. https://www.classicist.org/articles/classical-comments-bucrania/

58   James Yates, "Dolabra," in William Smith, *A Dictionary of Greek and Roman Antiquities* (John Murray, London, 1875) p. 420;

59 David Soren, *Malaria, Witchcraft, Infant Cemeteries and the Fall of Rome* (San Diego State University Department of Classics and Humanities 4-13-2002) pp. 11-12. On the fear of child-killing demons in early Italy see Titel Paule p. 65. See also Debbie Felton in footnote 71 below.

60 Several of the children exhibited something known as porotic hyperostosis which appears frequently in the presence of malaria. Porotic hyperostosis (*cribra orbitalia*) is a pathological condition that affects bones of the cranial vault, and is characterized by localized areas of spongy or porous bone tissue. As a result the spongy tissue within the bones of the cranium swells and distorts the appearance as the tissue of the outer surface becomes thinner and more porous in appearance. However, porotic hyperostosis does not only appear in the presence of malaria as has been demonstrated from repeated sampling. Nicole E. Smith-Guzman, "The skeletal manifestation of malaria: An epidemiological approach using documented skeletal collections," *American Journal of Biological Anthropology* 7-24-2015; Alvie Loufouma Mbouaka, Michelle Gamble, Christina Wurst, Heidi Yoko Jäger, Frank Maixner, Albert Zink, Harald Noedl & Michaela Binder, " The elusive parasite: comparing macroscopic, immunological, and genomic approaches to identifying malaria in human skeletal remains from Sayala, Egypt (third to sixth

centuries AD),” *Archaeological and Anthropological Sciences* volume 13, Article number: 115 (2021).

61 Christian Laes, “The Educated Midwife in the Roman Empire, An Example of Differential Equations,” in Manfred Horstmanshoff, *Hippocrates and Medical Education. Studies in Ancient Medicine Vol. 35* (Brill: Leiden, 2010) pp. 261-286; Lauren Hackworth Petersen, Patricia Salzman-Mitchell (editors), *Mothering and Motherhood in Ancient Greece and Rome* (University of Texas Press: Austin, 2012)

62- Valerie French, “Midwives and Maternity Care in the Ancient World,” in *Rescuing Creusa: New Methodological Approaches to Women in Antiquity, (Helios, New Series 13(2) Special Issue 1986),* pp. 69-84. On the education of midwives in Rome see Christian Laes, “The Educated Midwife in the Roman Empire: An Example of differential Equations,” in Manfred Horstmanshoff (editor), *Hippocrates and Medical Education. Studies in Ancient Medicine Vol. 35* (Brill: Leiden 2010) pp. 261-286. On Pliny’s alleged cures for the disease later identified as malaria, see Laura D. Lane, “Malaria: medicine and magic in the Roman world,” in Soren and Soren 1999 pp. 633-652.

63- *Gyn.*1.2.4.

64- René S. Bloch, *Ancient Jewish Diaspora: Essays on Hellenism* (Brill: Leiden, 2022) p. 42 citing the work of Fritz Graf. For the lack of the importance of the *magus* and magic itself in early Rome see also Justin J. Meggitt, “Did Magic Matter? The Saliency of Magic in the Early Roman Empire” *Journal of Ancient History*, vol. 1, no. 2, 2013, pp. 170-229. On how *sagae* were viewed in ancient Rome, see Pauline Ripat, “Roman Women, Wise Women and Witches,” *Phoenix* Vol. 70 pp. 104-128.

65- Luisa Migliorati, Ivana Fiore, Antonella Pansini, Paola Francesca Rossi, Tiziana Sgrulloni, Alessandra Sperduti, “Sepolti nel teatro: il valore simbolico dei cani in sepolture communi infantile,” *Scienze dell’Antichità*, Università di Roma, La Sapienza 23 (3) 2017 pp. 593-611. Sarah Iles Johnston has suggested in a personal communication that the dogs sacrificed here may have been intended as offerings to birth goddesses.

66- Hontos Iovios was apparently an agricultural god to whom puppies were sacrificed at the Hondia festival, as indicated on Iguvian Tablet II. Hontos Iovios is believed to have strong chthonic connections and the name Hontos is believed to mean “underworld” in Umbrian (Aldo Luigi Prosdocimi “L’Umbro,” in A. L. Prosdocimi, *Lingue e dialetti dell’ Italia antica* (Popoli e civiltá 1. Italia antica VI) Roma e Padova 1978 a cura di A. L. Prosdocimi pp. 713-717; 761-762).

67- Even today belief in what many perceive as established scientific fact is disputed by almost half of the population in the United States which believes in the supernatural. According to a 2019 YouGuv survey 45% of Americans currently believe in the existence of ghosts and demons.

68- One example is Julia, the daughter of emperor Augustus, and another is Tullia, the daughter of Cicero. On the hazards of childbirth and the need for midwives see Donald Todman, “Childbirth in ancient Rome: From traditional folklore to obstetrics,” *Australian and New Zealand Journal of Obstetrics and Gynaecology* 47 (2) pp. 82–85.

69- On the difficulty of Latin vocabulary in determining what is a demon or a witch, see Teitel Paule chapter 1.

70- Libations for the dead in ancient Greece were known as *nephalia* (νηφάλια). In Homer's *Odyssey*, Odysseus digs an offering pit to chthonic deities around which he pours, in order, honey, wine, and water. *Odyssey* 11.1-6

71- Debbie Felton, "Witches, Disgust and Anti-Abortion Propaganda in Imperial Rome, in Donald Lateiner, Dimos Spatharos (editors), *The Ancient Emotion of Disgust* (Oxford Scholarship Online, November, 2016) pp. 189-202 in which the stigma attached to aborted fetuses in ancient Rome is discussed as well as the perceived predilection of witches to attack fetuses and infants.

72- Horace, *Epode* V.17-20

73- Horace, Epode V.70-74

74- Horace, Epode V.87-94

75- *Plasmodium falciparum* malaria is spread by what are commonly termed night-biting mosquitoes, meaning that they appear between sunset and sunrise to do their biting. Source: National Health Service of Scotland. Although the ancient Romans would not have known that mosquitoes were spreading the disease, they may have realized that it is during the onset of darkness that it is actually transmitted.

76- Christopher Michael McDonough, "Carna, Proca and the Strix on the Kalends of June," *Transactions of the American Philological Association* 27 1997) 315-344; Ovid *Fasti* 6.101-182 tells a story in the time of the Alban kings of a five day old crown prince attacked by multiple *striges*, against which the sacrifice of a piglet was offered, its viscera left out for the creatures, and the child's health returning after a ceremony with an arbutus branch and sprinkled water.

77- Horace, *Epode* V.19-20

78- Plautus, *Pseudolus (The Cheat)* 3.2

79- *Fasti* VI. 159-162; On the *strix* in general see Daniel Ogden, The *Strix-Witch* (Cambridge University Press, 2021)

80- Ovid, *Fasti* VI.132. If you live in the foothills of southern Arizona and have western screech owls living under your eaves as many do, you can have the effect of being warned away by their shrieking when you approach them as they rotate their entire heads and stare you down.

81- Laura Cherubini, "The Virgin, The Bear, The Upside-Down Strix: An interpretation of Antoninus Liberalis 21," *Arethusa* Vol. 42, No. 1 (Winter 2009) pp. 77-97.

82- Montgomery, James A.. "The Lilith Legend." *The Museum Journal* IV, no. 2 (June, 1913): 62-65; Paule 2018 pp. 55-57 with detailed bibliography.

83- Dominique Collon *(2005). The Queen of the Night. British Museum Objects in Focus.* (London: British Museum Press, 2005); Pauline Albenda, "The 'Queen of the Night' Plaque: A Revisit". *Journal of the American Oriental Society. American Oriental Society.* 125 (2) 2005 pp. 171–190.

84- Johnston 1999 p. 174, note 30. Hana Šedinová, "The 'Lamia' and Aristotle's Beaver: The Consequences of a Mistranscription" *Journal of the Warburg and Courtauld Institutes,* Vol. 78, No. 1 2016) pp. 295-306; David Water Leinweber, "Witchcraft and Lamiae in 'The Golden Ass'", *Folklore* 105 (1-2) 1994 pp. 77-82; see also Diodorus Siculus 20.41 for the Lamia as a child devourer; David Walter Leinweber, "Witchcraft and "Lamiae" in *The Golden Ass*", *Folklore* 105 1994 pp. 77-82.

85- Sarah Iles Johnston, "Here Lies Hecate: Poetry and Apotheosis in Second-Century Mesembria," *Archiv für Religionsgeschichte* Vol. 24 (No. 1) 2023 pp.305-317 and especially 314; Sarah Iles Johnston, "Crossroads." *Zeitschrift für Papyrologie und Epigraphik* 88 (1991) p. 218. For a case of a mortal woman merged into the goddess Hecate herself, see Colleen Kron, "How to Become Immortal and Ageless: Affording Belief in Epitaphs with Extraordinary Claims," *Archiv für religionsgeschichte*, vol.24, no. 1 2023 pp. 281-303.

86- Nerea López Carrasco, "The Conception of the Goddess Hecate in Plutarch," *Brill's Plutarch Studies* Vol. 6 (Leiden) 2020 pp. 256-285 discusses the evolution of the goddess from Hesiod through Plutarch; Patricia A. Marquardt, "A Portrait of Hecate," *The American Journal of Philology*, Vol. 102 (no. 3) 1981 pp. 243-260.

87- Special thanks to Sarah Iles Johnston for her help in understanding the complexities of the Hecate cult. Johnston 1991 p. 218: "She eventually became associated ever more closely with the ghosts themselves, for a mistress who could keep them at bay could also lead them on, and in her wrathful, unsupplicated moments give them free rein to wreak terror."

88- Johnston 1999 p. 206.

89- James B. Rivas, "Magic in Roman Law: The Reconstruction of a Crime," Classical Antiquity 22 (2) 2003 pp. 317-322 on the *Lex Cornelia de Sicariis et Venefiis* of 81 B.C. under the dictator Sulla which took aim at poisoners and spell casters among other acts practiced by magicians. It was a law specifically against murderers and poisoners and shows the extent to which the practice of magic and spell casting was prevalent even at this time.

90- Paule 2018 pp. 14-16

91- Stefan Tilg, *Apuleius' Metamorphoses: A Study in Roman Fiction* (Oxford Scholarship Online, 2014) Chapter 8

92- Regine May, "Courtroom Drama: Apuleius'*Apologia*," in Regine May, *Apuleius and Drama: The Ass on Stage* (Oxford Scholarship Online, 2006) pp. 73-108

93- Apuleius, *Metamorphoses* Chapter 2 and especially 21-30.

94- Diodorus Siculus IV.45.2 discusses the lineage of Hecate; see also Paule 2008 pp. 43-44

95- Lucan *Pharsalia* 6.413-774

96- Lucan *Pharsalia* 6.651

97- Lucan *Pharsalia* 6.507

98- Lucan, *Pharsalia* 6.566-568; A. S. Kline translation.

99- Sarah Iles Johnston, "Defining the Dreadful: Remarks on the Greek Child-Killing Demon," in Marvin W. Meyer,. and Paul Allan Mirecki, (eds.), *Ancient Magic and Ritual Power (1995)* pp. 361–387; For various demons with similar characteristics, see Johnston 1999 pp. 161-199.

100-Johnston 1999 p. 164

101-Aristophanes *Frogs* 293f. in a comic reference claims that the shapeshifting *empousa* had one bronze leg and one made of cow dung! On this see Christopher G. Brown, "Empousa, Dionysus and the Mysteries: Aristophanes, *Frogs* 285ff.", *Classical Quarterly* 41 1991 pp. 41-50. Johnston 1999 pp. 133-134 discusses the root of *empousa* and determines it to be someone who impedes or blocks progress of others towards religious initiation or purification. She also gives full sourcing for the Hecate connection. See Teitel Paule 2018 pp. 108- 137

102-An *empousa* was thought to be able to be driven out by the use of *aischrologia* which were insults apparently shouted at it. On this see Paule 2018) pp. 124-125 who reports (page 78) on keeping away the *strix* through ritual sacrifices or incantations. A purple band on the *toga praetexta,* a toga worn by boys until they reached manhood, also was effective, in that it asserted the inviability of childhood; See also S. Sergio Ingallini, *Orazio e la magia* (Palumbo: Palermo, 1974) pp. 109-115 for a discussion of the confiscation by the witches of the presumed apotropaic *bulla* or protective amulet of the captured boy in Horace, *Epode* V.11-12.

103-Plutarch *Quaest. Rom.* 52,277a. On the attitude of young mothers facing giving birth, see now Anna Bonell Freiden, *Birthing Romans: Childbearing and Its Risks in Imperial Rome* (Princeton University Press, 2024)

104-Tertullian. *Ad Nationes* ii, 11. On the magical nature of the candle to reflect the hoped-for life of the newborn, see Eli Edward Burriss, *Taboo, Magic, Spirits: A Study of Primitive Elements in Roman Religion* (1931; Create Space/Amazon reprint, 2015), p. 34. Well into the Christian period, candlelight was used to illuminate icons in children's rooms to drive away the *gello* demon in Greece. For this, Karen Hartnup, *On the Beliefs of the Greeks: Leo Allatios and Popular Orthodoxy* (Brill, 2004), p. 95.

105-Daniel Ogden, *Magic, Witchcraft, and Ghosts in the Greek and Roman Worlds: A Sourcebook* (Oxford Univ. Press, 2002); Debbie Felton, *Haunted Greece and Rome: Ghost Stories from Classical Antiquity* (University of Texas Press: Austin, 1999); Antonio Stramaglia, *Res inauditae, incredulae: Storie di fantasmi nel mondo greco-latino* (Levante Editore: Bari 1999)

106-On the Edict of Milan of A.D. 313, see Willis G. Swartz, "The Early Church Persecution of Paganism and Heresy, *Social Science* Vol. 2, No. 2 1927 pp. 135-142; Alan Cameron, *The Last Pagans of Rome* (Oxford Academic Press, 2010)

107-Sarah Iles Johnston, *Hekate Soteira: A Study of Hekate's Roles in the Chaldean Oracles and Related Literature* (Oxford University Press, 1990) discusses this attribute in terms of theurgists, but inscriptions implying a more universal aspect for Hecate Soteira may be found in the following sources: Theodora Suk Fong Jim, *Saviour Gods and Soteria in Ancient Greece* (Oxford University Press, 2022) Appendix III: Hecate Soteira in Epitaphs. See also Murat Aydas, "New

Inscriptios from Stratonikeia and Its Territory," available online at https://www.acarindex. com/pdfler/acarindex-1452-6040.pdf15. He cites an inscription (number 15) to Hekate Soteira Epiphanes the great local goddess on behalf of the deified Julius Caesar and dating to 42 B.C. or soon after. On the great importance of the goddess' cult and influence in the Hellenistic period in this area see Christina G. Williamson, *Urban Rituals in Sacred Landscapes in Hellenistic Asia Minor* (Brill: Leiden 2021) chapter 5 on Festival Networks and The Sanctuary of Hekate at Lagina (Caria).

108-On the dog star see W. S. Burriss, *Animal Curiosities* (Boston, 1923) p. 99. On *seiriasis*, an inflammation of the membranes of the brain accompanied by burning fever which was considered a typical ailment of the *caniculae* or dog days of summer, see Soranus, *Gynaecology* 2.55. Pliny the Elder (*Hist. Nat.* 30.135) says that a treatment for this disease is and especially for infants suffering from inflammation from it is to use bone bits found in dog excrement and to wear them as an amulet. Those afflicted during the dog days or the *atrox hora caniculae* or horrible time of the little dog and the rise of Sirius were said to be *astrobletos* or star-struck. On Sirius causing actual heat illness see Hesiod, *Works and Days* 582-588.